The KingdomNomics Converterlator

Transforming Today's Opportunities into Eternal Treasure

By Phil Wiegand

Copyright © 2015 by KingdomNomics Foundation, Inc.

The KingdomNomics Converterlator
by Phil Wiegand

Printed in the United States of America.

ISBN 9781498447904

All rights reserved solely by the author. The author guarantees all contents are original and do not infringe upon the legal rights of any other person or work. No part of this book may be reproduced in any form without the permission of the author. The views expressed in this book are not necessarily those of the publisher.

Scripture quotations taken from the New International Version (NIV). Copyright © 1973, 1978, 1984, 2011 by Biblica, Inc.™. Used by permission. All rights reserved.

www.kingdomnomics.com

www.xulonpress.com

*In a race everyone runs,
but only one person gets first prize.
So run your race to win.
To win the contest
you must deny yourselves many things
that would keep you from doing your best.
An athlete goes to all this
trouble just to win a blue ribbon or a silver cup,
but we do it for a heavenly reward that
never disappears.*

−1 Corinthians 9:24–25, TLB

Contents

Acknowledgments ix
Introduction xiii
PART 1: ETERNAL PERSPECTIVE
  1 From Convert to Converterlator 17
  2 From Perishable to Imperishable 29
  3 From Consuming to Converterlating 43
  4 The Compass of Life 55
PART 2: TRANSFORMATION
  5 Your Relationship with God 69
  6 Trusting God in All Things 81
  7 Soaking Our Minds in God's Word 93
  8 Sowing God's Word 107
  9 Letting the Spirit Flow 119
PART 3: CONVERTERLATION
  10 You've Been Designed by God for
      a Purpose! 135
  11 Converterlating Your Time 151
  12 Converterlating Your Talent 165
  13 Converterlating Your Treasure 181
  14 Your Echo into Eternity 193
Appendix A: *KingdomNomics* DNA 201
Appendix B: *KingdomNomics* Gospel
          Presentation 203
More Resources and Phil's Bio 211

Acknowledgments

Bringing a book to print is no easy task! It takes many different individuals with many different talents to make sure that the ideas conveyed are clear and concise. I am passionate about *KingdomNomics* principles and am grateful to have a team around me that is committed to helping me communicate these important concepts in a wide variety of ways.

As always, I want to thank my wife, Ruth Ann, for encouraging me to speak and write about the principles that we have attempted to practice over the years on a daily basis.

I give a special expression of appreciation to Helmut Teichert who once again acted as the project manager for one of my books. Without his organization and recruitment of the team, all of the principles presented here would still be an eclectic mix of ideas sitting on my desk.

I am very thankful that Sheryl Moon was brought into this project to help with the writing in a way that only God could have orchestrated.

To those of you who have offered insight and ideas through the various drafts of the manuscript, please accept my heartfelt appreciation and gratitude. God has used your time and your talent to make this a better book and to hopefully help many more people become *KingdomNomics* Converterlators.

INTRODUCTION

Okay, you caught me! Until the writing of this book there was no such word as *Converterlator*. I created the word to describe the change that occurs in the life of a child of God who is shifting the gears of their life from *park* to *drive*. This transformation propels them into a life of *converterlating* and brings positive change into their lives from both an earthly and eternal standpoint. The purpose for doing so brings glory to our Creator God as we live an exciting and fulfilling life here on earth *and* build treasure for ourselves in heaven. This is a key principle of *KingdomNomics:* living a disciplined life committed to experiencing maximum returns in life *and* eternity.

Every human being born into this world is facing two undeniable facts. The first is that we are in this world for a brief period of time and then we face a physical death. The second is that each one of us will live in eternity. We will enter it either to be in the presence of God, or we will be eternally separated from him ... forever.

Our eternal destiny is determined by the relationship we have with God the Father through his Son, Jesus Christ. In the meanwhile, we have a life to live here on earth! The Bible is our guide in how we should not only live our lives here on earth, using our time, talent, and treasure for God's glory, but also how we should prepare for entering the world that will last forever.

In my first book, *KingdomNomics*, I discussed the importance of being wise stewards of all the resources God has given us: time, talent, and treasure. The purpose of this book is to delve into biblical principles in order to clarify how we are agents of change in this world with rewards in heaven for all that we accomplish here on earth using those resources.

The message contained in the following pages will only make sense for the person who has a relationship with God through Jesus Christ alone. It is important to understand that *what* we do (our works) in this world after we come to know Christ, impacts *how* we will live in the world to come. Christ not only came into this world to change *where* we will spend our eternal destiny, which is achieved when we put our trust in him as our personal Lord and Savior, but *how* we will spend eternity, which is impacted by what we do with the resources he has made available to us.

The Bible is clear that we will experience *rewards* in heaven. As I have used my time, talent, and treasure for God's kingdom, I have experienced a life of excitement, opportunity, impact, and what I know is going to be a legacy. I've written this book to help you experience the same thing! Take your life from *park* to *drive* and let your life echo into eternity.

PART 1
ETERNAL PERSPECTIVE

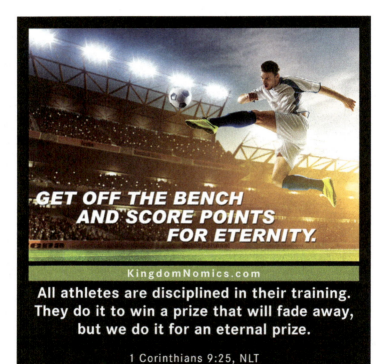

1

FROM CONVERT TO CONVERTERLATOR

So we fix our eyes not on what is seen, but on what is unseen, since what is seen is temporary, but what is unseen is eternal.
—2 Corinthians 4:18

God is in the life-changing business. You know that, right? And he wants to transform you into being more Christ-like in *all* areas of your life. The first step occurs when you place your faith in Christ alone to be your personal Lord and Savior. But accepting Jesus into your life is still only the first step. It is like getting *into* your car. Once you're *in*, you need to shift the gear from *park* to *drive!* You're not supposed to just sit there! It is important to understand that each one of us is supposed to be an agent of change; a transformer who not only experiences a life of joy now, but who also makes decisions that will make our life echo into eternity.

This is a basic principle of *KingdomNomics*: We use the resources available to us, what I like to refer to as the "three T's," time, talent, and treasure, to make a difference for eternity. And in so doing, we are *Converterlator*s.

> **A *Converterlator* actively uses their time, talent, and treasure to make a difference for eternity.**

A Converterlator is *actively working* to bring about kingdom change. A Converterlator understands God's purposes for giving us time, talent, and treasure to *use for him*. A Converterlator sees the big picture, a picture that is bigger than just life here on earth.

ACTIVELY CONVERTERLATING

When someone becomes a "convert," they profess faith in Jesus Christ as their Lord and Savior. As we read through the New Testament, we discover that there is an expectation that repentance for sin brings about a desire for holy living for those who profess their faith in Jesus Christ.

Unfortunately, for some professed believers forgiveness of their sin is where it all stops. They become *coasters*. Yes, they intellectually believe that Jesus died for their sin and is the way to a new relationship with God. However, their intellectual belief doesn't translate into anything meaningful. They live their lives in this way: "I made a decision for Christ, now I can go on living life for my own pleasure until I die."

Other believers become *doers*. These people make a decision for Christ and jump into doing good deeds related to the kingdom, *but* they spend little or no time in the Word of God. They have great intentions, but they are not grounded in God's purposes. And because they know so little about God's Word, they quite often have no understanding of the work or role or power of the Holy Spirit.

Still another group of believers become *observers*. Yes, they also have made a decision for Jesus Christ, and they may even be faithful in going to Bible studies and conferences. They have a lot of "head knowledge" of the Scripture, but that knowledge fails to move from their heads into their hearts so it has an impact on their *relationship* with God and others.

Finally, there are those who truly are transformed by their relationship with God through Jesus Christ and who are motivated by their knowledge of the Bible to become change agents in our world. These are the *Converterlators!* These people experience a living relationship with God that makes an impact in our world *and* for eternity. The Word of God plays the priority role in the lives of these people. It is impacting how they live and make decisions. Converterlators have learned how to tap into the power of the Holy Spirit and they are empowered in their everyday living. They practice living this verse on a daily basis: "My old self has been crucified with Christ. It is no longer I who live, but Christ lives in me. So I live in this earthly body by trusting in the Son of God, who loved me and gave himself for me" (Galatians 2:20, NLT). They are using their time, talent, and treasure for kingdom purposes. They understand what it means to have the DNA of a *KingdomNomics* thinker (for an overview of *KingdomNomics* DNA, see appendix A on page 203).

It is important to note here that in all other religions people attempt to reach God through works of self-effort, trusting in themselves and their own abilities. As Christ-followers, our "works" do not *bring us into* a relationship with God; they *flow out of* our relationship with him. Only Christ can live through us, because we do not have power in and of ourselves. When we establish a relationship with God we will find our attitudes changing. Our worldview changes as we begin to realize we need to think in terms of converting our resources into treasure for the kingdom in the world to come.

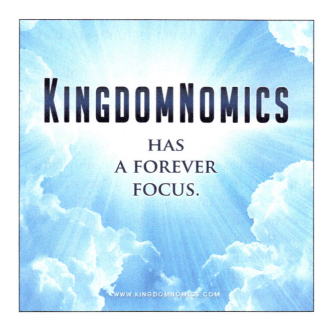

ON THE TEAM

When my son was only six, my wife and I decided it would be good for him to play in the children's recreational soccer league. Even at this young age, we found there were some requirements that needed to be met in order for him to be a member of the team.

First, we had to produce a birth certificate to prove his age. There were actually parents who tried to have their older children play on a younger team so their child could be a "star." They didn't really have eligibility to play.

Once our son had established eligibility to play, he had to make a commitment to attend practices, follow the rules of the game, play under the direction of the coach, wear the team uniform, and play with his team.

Those early games were great to watch! Some members of the team were on the sidelines having no interest in what was really happening. Other members were totally invested, wanting their time to play as soon as possible. Some team members didn't have much experience and just didn't know what to do. One player even kicked the ball in the wrong direction! Some of the players simply ran in the direction in which the ball was moving, but they weren't really watching the ball.

Even though those kids were on the soccer team, there were still many lessons to be learned. It takes a set of skills and organized teamwork to move the ball across the goal line to score points. Just running around and kicking the ball on the field will not accomplish anything. In those early games, my son had a great time, but very few points were scored.

KEY QUESTIONS

There is a reason Paul uses an athletic metaphor in 1 Corinthians 9:25, "All athletes are disciplined in their training. They do it to win a prize that will fade away, but we do it for an eternal prize" (NLT). There are a lot of crossover lessons from the world of sports to our lives as Christians!

Just as you must have eligibility when joining a sports team, you must have "eligibility" to be on "God's team." There are some who are supposedly on the team, actually wearing the uniform, who are not eligible to be on the team from a spiritual standpoint. They do not have the "birth certificate" acknowledging they are true believers who are trusting in the person of Jesus Christ, alone, for their salvation. This is the first question each person must ask of themselves: *Am I truly a member of the team?*

And in order to answer that question, you need to answer "yes" to this question: *Have I accepted Jesus Christ as my Lord and Savior?* When we accept the salvation of Jesus Christ, we establish our relationship with God the Father. We are now ready to actually begin to go to practice! (If your answer to this question is "no" or even "I'm not sure," see appendix B on page 205.)

And just as my son had to attend practices, follow the rules of the game, play under the direction of the coach, wear the team uniform, and play with the team, we need to attend practices (in whatever form that may be for you such as worship, classes, and Bible studies), follow the rules of the game (found in the Bible!), play under the direction of the Ultimate Coach (God), wear the team uniform (Christian character), and play with the team (other Christians). Many people refuse to listen to the "coach" or fail to show up for practice in order to be properly trained. A sense of purpose and training is required to be an effective team player on the church team. Each player has a role to play. Each player is needed to fill a position. Each player has to work with the other players in order for the points to be scored. We need to understand the game and know our own position. And so the next question is: *What am I doing as a member of this team?*

Then there is the matter of being on the "field of play." How many people do you know who are content to "sit the bench"? They go to practice, but they never play! There are others who are totally invested in the team, and are simply waiting for an opportunity to present itself to them. And then there are those team members who don't yet have much experience and don't know what to do. It costs something to be a team player in this game. Yes, just as in the athletic world there is the saying, "Without pain, there is no gain," the same is true in the "game" we are playing with God ... but the stakes are much higher than a win or loss.

Anything worthwhile costs something. However, the benefits of being a playing member in *this* game far outweigh any of the costs involved. After all, we are talking about scoring *eternal* points here. Even in this world, the quality of life and benefits for the active believer far exceed those in the life of the inactive one. And so we come to this question: *What am I doing on the field of play?*

> **Anything worthwhile costs something.**

And once you are on the field of play, there is the matter of playing by the rules of the game. Many Christians today say they know and understand the rules of the game; however, they rarely or never pick up the playbook, the Bible, and read the instructions

God has given so they will know how to play the game successfully.

Playing in *this* game is far different than playing in any other game in this world. In fact, we will find that many of the "rules" for playing in God's game are directly opposite from the rules followed by the world in achieving the goals highly exalted by man. It is one thing to *know* about a truth; it is quite another to actually *experience* that truth. Only the Bible can provide us with the answers to our questions about direction and purpose. This brings us to the next question you must ask yourself: *Am I taking time regularly to delve into the contents of the Bible, so I can know, understand, and experience the life God wants to impart to me while I am in this world?*

Okay, let's assume you meet all the qualifications and conditions mentioned above. You are an eligible member of the team. You understand the rules for playing the game. You know the position you are supposed to play, and even how to play it. You are even on the field of play. The next key question is: *Am I helping to move the ball in the right direction ... from an eternal perspective?*

And that brings us precisely to the contents of this book. We want to make sure we are strategically using our time, talent, and treasure for God's kingdom while we are in this world.

We want to strategically use our time, talent, and treasure for God's kingdom while we are in this world.

A MATTER OF FOCUS

There are many good causes and worthwhile objectives. We want to focus on the ones that have eternal value, on results that will last forever. Everything we do or do not do has an eternal impact. When it comes to this world, we are just passing through. And so, I want to enjoy the life God has given to me, and at the same time keep my focus on the eternal life to come.

The Converterlator wants God's seal of approval on his life more than anything else. He makes sure his car is in *drive* and on the move. He wants to make sure he "gets off the bench," and becomes a high impact player on the field. Life is too short to just be a spectator. Plus, it is a lot more fun to be playing on the field!

Convert to Converterlator:

Ask yourself these questions:

- Am I living my Christian life as a *coaster, observer, doer, or Converterlator*? If I am not living as a *Converterlator*, what changes do I need to make to become one?
- Am I truly a member of God's team? Have I accepted Jesus Christ as my Lord and Savior? (See appendix B on page 205.)
- What am I doing as a member of God's team? What am I doing on the field of play?
- Am I taking time regularly to delve into the contents of the Bible, so I can know,

understand, and experience the life God wants to impart to me while I am in this world?
- Am I scoring points ... from an eternal perspective?
- In what ways am I a *Converterlator;* using my "three T's" (time, talent, and treasure) for kingdom purposes?

2

FROM PERISHABLE TO IMPERISHABLE

Do not work for the food that perishes, but for the food that endures to eternal life, which the Son of Man will give to you.

—John 6:27, ESV

Have you ever considered that *everything* you and I can see and touch is ultimately going to pass away? We live in a *perishable* world; it is all subject to decay and destruction. That's a sobering thought! However, the things of heaven are imperishable; they will last forever! And we can store up our true treasure in heaven.

Jesus said, "But store up for yourselves treasures in heaven, where neither moth nor rust destroys, and where thieves do not break in or steal" (Matthew 6:20, NASB). Do you want to be rich in the next world, the real world, the world that will last forever? If so, you need to be actively converterlating the perishable items of this world into the imperishable treasures of the world to come.

Converterlators understand that we all live in a time bubble that can pop in this perishing world at any time. When that happens we will find ourselves in a totally different paradigm. The wise person realizes that in the end, all of our earthly time, talent, and treasure is going to perish. The apostle Paul made this point clear when he said, "For we brought nothing into the world, and we can take nothing out of it" (1 Timothy 6:7). Think of it, everything we know and love about this world will eventually be *gone*!

> **We need to be converterlating the perishable items of this world into the imperishable treasure of the world to come.**

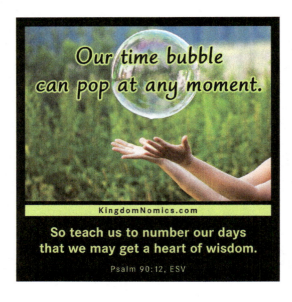

This eternal focus was at the core of Paul's teaching. He set his eyes and his heart on the eternal because he knew that the world as we know it is temporary and wasting away. Paul's eyes were fixed on eternity, and he conducted his life accordingly.

Each one of us has to make a choice: Do we want to enjoy life within the Lord's framework so our lives can echo into eternity, or are we going to live our lives dedicated to the temporary values of this perishing world?

As we study the Bible, we discover we are in the middle of two totally different value systems that are striving to win our commitment and loyalty. The first is what we call the perishable world system, and the second is the imperishable eternal realm. Paul tells us,

> Command those who are rich in this present world not to be arrogant nor to put their hope in wealth, which is so uncertain, but to put their hope in God, who richly provides us with everything for our enjoyment. Command them to do good, to be rich in good deeds, and to be generous and willing to share. In this way they will lay up treasure for themselves as a firm foundation for the coming age, so that they may take hold of the life that is truly life.
> —1 Timothy 6:17–19

The world system is doing everything it can to consume all of our temporary time, talent, and treasure, enticing us to invest all of them into stuff, activity, and experiences that in the end of life will have no eternal value. For the most part, the world system is held together by force, greed, and power. It caters to developing a self-centered life, a self-first mindset; it is bent on finding significance in power, fame, status, and accumulation of wealth. A wrong emphasis on these things often destroys the lives of people and their loved ones.

Self, fame, status, personal wealth: these often become idols in the lives of many people, even those who profess to have a relationship with God through Jesus Christ. These things take the place that God should have in our lives. In many instances the world system emphasizes striving to get more for doing less. Get as much stuff as you can so you can retire from work and have a life of ease doing what you want to do when you want to do it. It does everything it can to keep us from thinking about the eternal aspect of life.

On the other hand, we have the value system of the heavenly realm revealed to us by the person of Jesus Christ emphasizing a life of love, giving, and serving. This involves work that leads to glorifying God, building treasure for oneself in the next world, and living a life of fulfillment in this world as well. Jesus Christ came into this world not only to save us from separation from God for *eternity*; he also came into the world to save us from wasting our lives while we are here in *this world*.

> **The value system of the heavenly realm is revealed to us by the person of Jesus Christ.**

TRUE PURPOSE

God intends for us to work while we are still in this world, "For we are his workmanship, created in Christ Jesus for good works, which God prepared beforehand, that we should walk in them" (Ephesians 2:10, ESV).

Everything you and I can see and touch is ultimately going to pass away. Our time, talent, and treasure from a value standpoint will expire when we do. In eternity they will do us no good. We are forced to spend and use them while we are here on this side of eternity. We are like the shopper who has won a contest and is allowed to buy as many groceries as she can within a short period of time. When the time expires, the shopping spree ends.

Gold and all worldly wealth are going to perish like everything else. The Bible tells us:

> They will throw their silver into the streets,
> And their gold will be like refuse;
> Their silver and their gold will not be able to deliver them
> In the day of the wrath of the Lord;
> They will not satisfy their souls,
> Nor fill their stomachs,
> Because it became their stumbling block of iniquity.
> —Ezekiel 7:19, NKJV

However, although all worldly wealth is going to perish, the Bible tells us that the Word of God will never pass away, and we also know that the soul of each person is going to exist forever in either heaven or hell. This is good news; we have the opportunity to make a difference beyond this perishing world!

Jesus said, "Here's the lesson: Use your worldly resources to benefit others and make friends. Then, when your earthly possessions are gone, they will welcome you to an eternal home" (Luke 16:9, NLT). I believe this is the Converterlator in action, investing in what counts for eternity. We are fishers of people, saving them from perishing and preparing them for new life in this world and a life in the imperishable world of eternity. We are making friends for eternity by converterlating our temporary, perishing time, talent, and treasure into eternal value!

> **We have the opportunity to make a difference beyond this perishing world!**

We are talking about *eternity* here, and it is important we try to understand what is at stake. In *KingdomNomics* we are concerned with the brevity of life. The Bible itself comments extensively on life and how short it is. One verse that sums up this thought is, "Why, you do not even know what will happen tomorrow. What is your life? You are a mist that appears for a little while and then vanishes" (James 4:14). We need to be busy converterlating the perishable into the imperishable before time expires. We want to be active Converterlators before the opportunity to do so vanishes!

THE PENNIES OF THIS WORLD

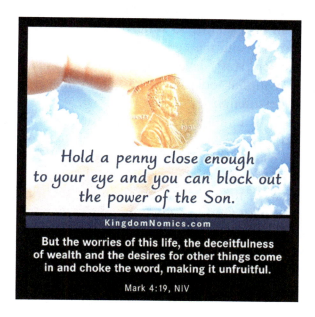

It's easy to be blinded by earthly wealth. One day I took a penny and held it very close to my eye, keeping the other eye closed. I found that if I held the penny close enough to my eye, I could block out the sun. In the same way, the pennies of this world can block out the power and life of Jesus Christ when we hold them too close.

Scripture has names for the things that are a barrier between us and God, "But the *worries of this life,* the *deceitfulness of wealth* and the *desires for other things* come in and choke the word, making it unfruitful" (Mark 4:19, emphasis added). These things can keep us from having the relationship God wants us to have with him. We fail to realize that, "one's life does not consist in the abundance of his possessions" (Luke 12:15, ESV). What a tragedy to spend all of one's life to simply please oneself with the currency and the "goods" of this world. Living life just for "stuff" is a big mistake. It can lead one on the road that looks so good, but ultimately leads to self-destruction.

There is nothing intrinsically wrong with things or money. However, we enter into the red zone of trouble when we look to them to provide life for us as a substitute for God in our lives. It is only through the prism of the Cross that we can see the true purpose for why God has given us our resources. We need to remember that our earthly resources have been given to us so that we can enjoy them *and* use them for eternal purposes along life's way. Yes, our resources can be used to accumulate treasure in heaven! How so? Let's look at the example of the wise men, "On coming to the house, they saw the child with his mother Mary, and they bowed down and worshiped him. Then they opened their treasures and presented him with gifts of gold, frankincense and myrrh" (Matthew 2:11). This act of worship will be remembered for all of eternity.

The wise person today will do the very same thing as the wise men did when they visited the young Jesus: use their talents to seek him, use their time to pursue him, and present their treasure to the King to be used for his purposes. This is the Converterlator in action, investing in what counts for eternity. The "smart money" is going into the kingdom of God. We want to be in the process of helping to save people from a purposeless eternity. We want to be about helping to prepare them for not only a new life in this world but a life in the imperishable world of eternity as well. We are making friends for eternity by converterlating our temporary, perishing time, talent, and treasure into eternal value. It actually makes "cents" for us to invest in the kingdom of God.

SHELF LIFE

Everything you and I can see, touch, and feel will perish someday. And yet, even in this world some things have a longer shelf life than others. Realization of this basic truth impacts the way in which we conduct our lives.

In case of some kind of community crisis, I have stored some extra foods that have an extended shelf life. When I do this, I do not store fresh fruits and vegetables. They are perishable items having a short shelf life of just a few days. It would be a waste of resources to do this. Instead, I look for items that have a much longer shelf life. Some canned goods can be stored for two to five years. Certain freeze-dried foods have a shelf life of twenty to twenty-five years! On a comparison basis, these items are considered almost imperishable in a practical sense if they are stored properly ... and yet, they are still perishable. They will have no value in eternity.

I have come to realize that whatever time, talent, and treasure I have in this world will lose their value when I leave this world. Because of this fact, they are perishable items. These will do me no good in the world to come. Their value only lasts while I am in this world. It was a lightbulb moment for me when I finally came to realize I was spending all of my time and effort on things that are in the process of perishing. Earthly objectives like careers, positions, status, wealth, physical fitness, accumulated "stuff," etc., are all perishable items. I really wasn't using any of my resources for God's kingdom. After I became a Christian, I learned that my spirit is going to last forever. It will only be spent in the presence of the Lord if I have established a right relationship with him.

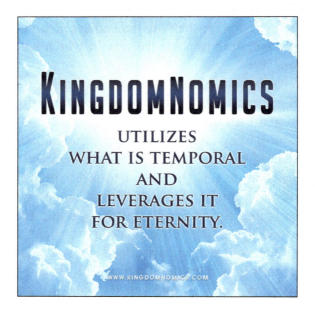

One of the tangible results of my reflection was my changed motivation for making money. Before encountering Christ, my philosophy was "make as much as I can and save as much as I can, so I can sit on my can someday." But as I began to study the Bible and understand God's plan for my life, my thinking took a totally new turn. I began to see myself as a "spiritual financial farmer," growing money with a mission. My goal became to "make as much as I can and save as much as I can so I can give away as much as I can for the advancement of God's kingdom."

The time, talent, and treasure we have are all perishable, but they become imperishable when we invest them in the kingdom of God; they last forever with ever-increasing eternal rewards.

THE REWARD FACTOR

The eternal rewards that we will someday receive should be a huge motivational factor in the life of the believer. The Bible is filled with verses that talk about our eternal reward.

> And now the prize awaits me—the crown of righteousness, which the Lord, the righteous Judge, will give me on the day of his return.
> —2 Timothy 4:8, NLT

> Anyone who builds on that foundation may use a variety of materials—gold, silver, jewels, wood, hay, or straw. But on the judgment day, fire will reveal what kind of work each builder has done. The fire will show if a person's work has any value. If the work survives, that builder will receive a reward. But if the work is burned up, the builder will

suffer great loss. The builder will be saved, but like someone barely escaping through a wall of flames.
—1 Corinthians 3:12–15, NLT

Look, I am coming soon! My reward is with me, and I will give to each person according to what they have done.
—Revelation 22:12

The time, talent, and treasure we have are all perishable, but they become imperishable when we invest them in the kingdom of God.

So here we are. We are living in a perishable world. We are going to a world that is imperishable. In the meantime we are to be preparing for the imperishable world by being engaged in a transformation process in this perishing world, "And we all, with unveiled face, beholding the glory of the Lord, are being transformed into the same image from one degree of glory to another. For this comes from the Lord who is the Spirit" (2 Corinthians 3:18, ESV). What Christ has done for us compels us to be focused on God's kingdom!

The game clock is running. What are you doing on the playing field to make a difference for all eternity?

Perishable to Imperishable:

Take some time to think about and answer these questions:

- Honestly, what are the *perishable* things in my life that are receiving my time, talent, and treasure?
- What *cares of the world* are currently consuming my time, talent, and treasure?
- In what ways am I trapped by the *deceitfulness of riches*?
- What *desires* in this world are keeping me from being fruitful for God's kingdom?
- What is one step I can take to focus more on the imperishable things of *God's kingdom*?
- How does what is in this chapter affect my understanding of being a Converterlator?

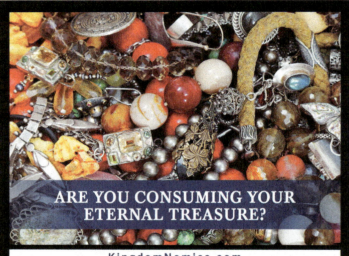

3

FROM CONSUMING TO CONVERTERLATING

The thief's purpose is to steal and kill and destroy. My purpose is to give them a rich and satisfying life.
—John 10:10, NLT

Way back in the Garden of Eden, Eve wanted what *she* wanted! God had told her and Adam that they could eat of *any* tree in the garden ... except for one. And Eve decided she wanted *more*. Satan came and enticed her; he convinced her that she wanted the fruit of *that* tree and the knowledge that he promised would come with it. She wanted *more* than what God had already given her.

Unfortunately, we are all in the same boat. Most of us want *more*. *More* of whatever we don't have. *More* stuff, *more* prestige, *more* opportunity, *more* power, *more* influence. You name it; we want more of it, if we're honest. And because of that desire for *more*, we concentrate on how we can meet our *own* desires and needs and give little thought to our eternal destinies or the eternal destinies of others. But you know what? God wants to change the propensity you have to focus on *yourself* into a focus on *his* desires and goals. Because when we focus on ourselves, we are willing to consume our time and talent and treasure on the immediate rather than invest it in the eternal.

THE CHIEF CONSUMERLATOR

The Bible tells us in Genesis 1–3 that God created a beautiful and perfect world. He created Adam and Eve in his image to inhabit his perfect world with the express purpose of having fellowship with him. And his creative design was for Adam and Eve to administer responsible stewardship over his creation.

Unfortunately, a fallen angel, named Lucifer, entered God's creation to entice mankind to disobey God, thereby introducing sin into God's perfect creation. We often refer to Lucifer as "Satan." Peter describes him in the New Testament in this way, "Your enemy the devil prowls around like a roaring lion looking for someone to devour" (1 Peter 5:8). I like to refer to Satan as the Chief Consumerlator (another new word!). A *consumerlator* is anyone or anything that steals an opportunity to converterlate time, talent, or treasure into something of eternal value. Satan's express purpose is always to steal, kill, and destroy that which is good. He will use whatever means possible to get us to use our resources on those things that are perishable. He wants us consuming our resources rather than converterlating them!

CHOICES, CHOICES, CHOICES

We have been born into a world not of our own making; it is a world full of conflict with many voices demanding our attention. Specific circumstances, including physical, emotional, mental, spiritual, and material, shape and influence our lives in almost unlimited ways. And the conflict rages in both the seen and unseen worlds; Ephesians 6:12 tells us, "For we are not fighting against flesh-and-blood enemies, but against evil rulers and authorities of the unseen world, against mighty powers in this dark world, and against evil spirits in the heavenly places" (NLT). Our world tells us, "Use this specific product, buy this specific brand, accumulate more stuff, desire the best, use your time here, use your talents there." And all the while, we are consuming. Only God's Word can give us the hope, power, and guidance we need to make our way through the jungle of activity in this complex world.

It is important to remember that the choices we make *now* impact greatly how we not only experience life here on earth, but how we will live in eternity. Second Corinthians 5:10 says, "For we must all stand before Christ to be judged. We will each receive whatever we deserve for the good or evil we have done in this earthly body" (NLT). This provides us with enormous opportunity! We need to embrace the fact that life now can be tons of fun when we become Converterlators!

STARTING WITH THE TRUTH OF GOD'S WORD

The Bible tells us:

> For no one can lay any foundation other than the one we already have—Jesus Christ. Anyone who builds on that foundation may use a variety of materials—gold, silver, jewels, wood, hay, or straw. But on the judgment day,

fire will reveal what kind of work each builder has done. The fire will show if a person's work has any value. If the work survives, that builder will receive a reward. But if the work is burned up, the builder will suffer great loss.
—1 Corinthians 3:11–15, NLT

The foundation for all converterlating is found in this verse; the Bible is clear that we begin our converterlating with our relationship with Jesus Christ! From there, it is critical that we learn to make the Word of God operative in our lives so we can make the right choices. God's Word gives us the wisdom we need to avoid the eternally devastating result of having our life end up in a pile of ashes.

It is critical that we learn to make the Word of God operative in our lives so we can make the right choices.

LOOKING BEYOND THE IMMEDIATE

We all know there are foolish ways and wise ways to spend our time, talent, and treasure. We can either consume our resources, using them for perishable pleasure, or use these resources for imperishable treasure. How do we stay focused? Psalm 32:8 tells us, "The Lord says, 'I will make you wise and show you where to go. I will guide you and watch over you'" (NCV). We need to ask for God's wisdom!

When Ruth Ann and I decided to marry, we had a limited period of time to make some major decisions.

I have found that a great many people spend an inordinate amount of time and money preparing for the wedding ceremony and for the reception that follows, and very little if any time is spent on counseling or exposure to the biblical teachings that will help to establish a firm foundation for a long-term marriage relationship.

Fortunately, both of us had a great deal of exposure to personal counseling as well as Bible study. Both the counseling and exposure to the Word of God gave us confidence that our marriage was the right thing to do. We found these two elements to be important for our relationship.

When taking the time to pursue counseling, it is interesting to note that sometimes people come to realize they should not enter the marriage relationship and they decide not to marry. This is a good use of time (and treasure, since counseling usually costs money)! Obviously, it is better to use a portion of the wedding funds for wise counsel; investing in the relationship itself, rather than simply consuming all of it on a temporary ceremony. A wedding is a one-time event, and as special as it is, it is over quickly. A marriage is for a life-time. Instead of having a marriage with a short "shelf life," the couple who wisely uses their money for something that will benefit them down the road has a better chance of experiencing a lasting marriage.

Another example of using treasure for the long term is the planning and investing for retirement. The bottom line: if all dollars are spent on immediate consumption, little is left over for proper investment to finance one's retirement. A very large percentage of Americans have inadequate funds to finance their retirement. It takes discipline and a denial to spend on immediate gratification in order to plan and invest for a future retirement.

I have tried to follow a basic principle through the years: I try to make as much as I can, save as much as I can, and give away as much as I can, *taking into account whatever financial obligations* I have. Here's where God's wisdom is critical. We can rationalize *anything*. It's important to enjoy the fruits of our labor within what we determine to be "reasonable," while at the same time staying sensitive to God's direction.

THE BEST DEFENSE IS A GOOD OFFENSE

The Bible tells us, "Sin is crouching at your door; it desires to have you, but you must rule over it" (Genesis 4:7). Since the beginning of time, Satan has been seeking to trip people up! It is critical that the resurrection power of Christ be at work in our lives in order to enable us to live the life that God desires for us. As this power grows in our hearts, the spiritual desires to invest our time, talent, and treasure in the kingdom of God will overcome our desires for pursuing perishable things. The lure of the world is constantly with us. We must find a way to recognize when we are being tempted to waste our resources, and then know what to do about it! When we submit to God, the Holy Spirit empowers us to focus on his desires for us.

What kind of legacy are we going to leave behind in this world when our time bubble pops? I remember a conversation with a friend about a mutual acquaintance who had passed away. My friend made the comment, "Man, did that guy ever like to party! The parties at his place were out of this world!" And I thought, "Wow, that is some legacy!" What benefit to the world was that? What benefit to the kingdom of God? Celebration is part of life, but to make it the only focus in life is a great mistake. Like every boat, your life will leave a wake behind it. The question is: *What kind of wake are you leaving behind?* What will those who knew you, say about you when you are gone? In the New Testament we read, "Demas has deserted me because he loves the things of this life" (2 Timothy 4:10, NLT). Demas apparently was unwilling to defer experiencing temporary pleasure in order to accumulate treasure in heaven. Being actively involved as a converterlator is one of the best protections against falling into the plight of Demas. When we engage in the things God has for us, we are less likely to become distracted by what the world has to offer.

Only the Word of God can give us a proper perspective. The world system ultimately destroys and will be destroyed itself according to Scripture. Even so, the Bible gives us the counsel we need to conduct ourselves in this difficult world. We have the opportunity to become skilled Converterlators. If we are successful in this endeavor, we will be victors rather than victims. Failure to become a skilled Converterlator means we run the risk of being devoured

> **What kind of legacy are you going to leave behind?**

by the Chief Consumerlator, causing us to suffer eternal loss.

We live in a world filled with conflict. Satan is doing his best to disrupt our lives and divert our attention from achieving the goals God has for us. As we read earlier in Ephesians 6:12, conflict rages in the spiritual realm. We see only a small part of the larger battle, but individually we experience this battle in a variety of ways, including physical, material, spiritual, emotional, and mental stresses. However, we do have a powerful weapon to counteract any attack we experience. The Word of God gives us the hope, power, and guidance we need to make our way through this complex world. "The Lord says, 'I will make you wise and show you where to go. I will guide you and watch over you'" (Psalm 32:8, NCV).

The KingdomNomics Converterlator

Jesus said we need to be wise as serpents, since we are in a world full of ravenous wolves (Matthew 10:16). The world system will ultimately destroy and be destroyed itself according to Scripture. Even so, the Bible provides the direction we need to make wise choices in this difficult world.

In Ephesians 6 we read, "Put on the full armor of God, so that you can take your stand against the devil's schemes. Stand firm then, with the belt of truth ... the breastplate of righteousness, ... your feet fitted with the readiness that comes from the gospel of peace ... take up the shield of faith ... the helmet of salvation and the sword of the Spirit, which is the Word of God" (verses 11–17). The Christian life is all about advancing for the purpose of accomplishing God's will on this earth. We invade the darkness with the light of the gospel, going into all the world with all of the means God has given us. Retreat is not an option. We are in a battle, taking new ground.

I took my son to the Gettysburg battlefield and we found a small plaque in the ground that said, "Write home, and tell them I died facing the enemy." This person *faced* the enemy, they did not retreat! The list of armor in Ephesians does not mention any protective provision for our back. We are to advance, not retreat! We are to invade our culture. We are to use our time, talent, and treasure to make a difference for the kingdom. We must be bold. We must be empowered by the Spirit.

Are you consuming all of your resources? Are you giving in to the enticement of the Chief Consumerlator? Put on God's armor and resist the temptations to fritter away God-given resources. Face the enemy with all of God's power and focus on his purpose for your life! Leave a legacy that will matter eternally.

Consuming to Converterlating:

Reflect on these questions:

- What am I consuming on a daily basis that is perishable?
- What am I presently converterlating for God's kingdom?
- How much of my time am I committing to the study of God's Word?
- What does the Chief Consumerlator most often use in my life to distract me from God's purposes?
- What part of my time, talent, or treasure do I need to immediately stop consuming for personal pleasure?
- If I continue on the same path, what kind of legacy will I leave behind in this world when my time bubble pops?
- What step do I need to take in order to be more intentional about converterlating my time, talent, and treasure into God's purposes?
- How can I best utilize God's armor in my own life?

4

THE COMPASS OF LIFE

But we have the mind of Christ.
—1 Corinthians 2:16

For a brief period of time in the early part of my business career, I was in a location where hunting was big on the agenda of most men. I grew up in the city, and I knew very little about hunting. My knowledge of how to manage myself in the woods was even less. I bought all of the necessary clothing, boots, thermal underwear, gloves, warm hat, and a compass. This was long before the days of having a portable GPS device available. To top off the list of purchases, I bought an advertised rifle by Remington that supposedly could kill anything on the North American continent. I was ready to go!

On a cold day in November, I joined a few other men who had experience in navigating their way through the woods of northwestern Pennsylvania for a hunting day. It was one of those days when it was *really* cold, and I lacked the endurance of some of the veterans who were able to tramp through the woods for hours at a time regardless of the weather conditions.

After a few hours of being outside, I told the guys that I was ready to call it quits. I pulled out my compass and unknowingly held it very close to the rifle barrel that was in my other hand. I told them I thought I should go in a particular direction back to where my car was located.

In the background I heard a few chuckles, and one of the men suggested that I move the compass away from the rifle barrel and see if the needle was still pointing in the same direction. When I did that, the needle snapped a full fifteen degrees in another direction! Wow! If I had followed the first reading, which was totally inaccurate due to my lack of knowledge, I would have lost my way in the woods and mountains.

There is a huge application here. As we delve into the pages of the Bible, we discover we are in the middle of two totally different value systems striving to win our commitment and loyalty. The one is the perishing world system, and the other is the imperishable eternal realm lasting forever. We need to be aware that the world system will always point us in the wrong direction.

THE RIGHT POINT OF REFERENCE

Using the right point of reference is critical in making our decisions in this world. If we do not have the right point of reference, we will lose our way in the vast complexity of this perishable world system. All of us face a myriad of voices bombarding us for the consummation of our time, talent, and treasure. Which ones should we listen to? Which path should we take when we come to a crossroads? Are there criteria for us to follow?

I believe the key question is: *Who is controlling my mind?* This is the battle ground. Whoever or whatever controls our mind controls us. The Converterlator seeks to have *Jesus Christ* control his mind, "For to set the mind on the flesh is death, but to set the mind on the Spirit is life and peace" (Romans 8:6, ESV). This is why the psalmist said, "My eyes are ever on the Lord, for only he will release my feet from the snare" (Psalm 25:15); and "I keep my eyes always on the Lord. With him at my right hand, I will not be shaken" (Psalm 16:8, ESV).

The world system will always point us in the wrong direction.

This truth brings us to the Compass of Life Concept. The *needle* of our life is our *mind*. In our mind we make the decisions, good or bad, that determine what we actually end up doing with our time, talent, and treasure.

Remember, we live in an environment held under the influence of the evil one, "We know that we are from God, and the whole world lies in the power of the evil one" (1 John 5:19, ESV). There is an automatic gravitational pull to the wrong direction that we need to overcome. The Chief Consumerlator will use whatever means possible to control our mind.

If we allow the needle of our lives to focus on the wrong reference point, we will end up making wrong decisions. We will also end up pursuing things that ultimately lead to death and destruction. So another critical question each one of us needs to ask is: *How do I decide what the right reference point is?*

THE COMPASS OF LIFE

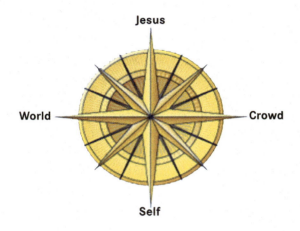

The diagram above illustrates a compass. If this was a typical compass, *north* would be at the top of the circle, *east* on the right side, *south* on the bottom of the circle, and *west* on the left side of the circle. However, this is not a typical compass! As you can see, we've substituted *Jesus* on the north point, *Crowd* on the east, *Self* on the south, and *World* on the west. These are the general reference points that strive to capture our attention and control the needle of our lives. But we possess a power that can exert influence over the needle.

We must *choose* to point our decision-making process in the right direction. If we fail to do so, we will be subject to consumerlating, frittering away our perishable commodities of time, talent, and treasure. When this happens, we lose our opportunities for converterlating them into the imperishable eternal values that will echo into eternity. We will end life in this world and start life in heaven with nothing!

> **Jesus Christ is the only true reference point.**

TRUE NORTH

What we want is to have Jesus Christ as the only true reference point of life. Jesus said, "I am the way and the truth and the life. No one comes to the Father except through me" (John 14:6). Jesus is the way, the truth, and the life. This statement of truth is directional: Jesus Christ is *True North* personified.

As we fix our eyes and thoughts on Jesus, we focus our mind on him. When we do so, we experience extreme benefits.

> Therefore, holy brothers and sisters, *who share in the heavenly calling*, fix your thoughts on Jesus, whom we acknowledge as our apostle and high priest.
> —Hebrews 3:1, emphasis added

> Fixing our eyes on Jesus, the pioneer and perfecter of faith. For the *joy* set before him he endured the cross, scorning its shame, and sat down at the right hand of the throne of God.
> —Hebrews 12:2, emphasis added

> For it is *God who works in you* to will and to act in order *to fulfill his good purpose*.
> —Philippians 2:13, emphasis added

> Trust in the Lord with all your heart; do not depend on your own understanding. Seek his will in all you do, and *he will show you which path to take*.
> —Proverbs 3:5–6, NLT, emphasis added

The greatest discovery we make when we plunge into the Bible is that our relationship with God through Christ is far more valuable than anything else this world has to offer. The living, vibrant relationship with God is life! Not only that, we obtain favor from the Lord! All of the promises of God find their "yes" of fulfillment in the person of Jesus Christ.

HEADING IN THE WRONG DIRECTION

First, let's consider *Self*, the southern point on the Compass of Life. The Bible says, "Those who trust in *themselves* are fools, but those who walk in wisdom are kept safe" (Proverbs 28:26, emphasis added). Without a proper reference point in life, we end up being a fool! This is an extremely strong statement,

The Compass of Life

and we want to avoid this label like the plague. The message is, "Do not trust in yourself for directing your steps in this world!" The needle of our minds must be focused on something other than on *Self*.

In the Old Testament, whenever people trusted in their own ideas and abilities, what was the result? The judgment of God! Over and over again, the people of Israel got themselves into trouble when they failed to let God direct them. One specific verse in Judges illustrates this: "In those days there was no king in Israel. Everyone did what was right in his own eyes" (Judges 21:25, ESV). *Self* is never the right reference.

Secondly, we have the *Crowd*, found on the compass illustration on the right side. The *Crowd* represents people we are trying to please, including peer pressure and our own desire to be accepted. One of the attitudes that pulls the needle in this direction is, "Everybody else is doing it, so it must be okay." When we follow the crowd, typically nothing worthwhile is accomplished.

In the New Testament we read about Zacchaeus, who dared to do something that made him stand out from the crowd. Zacchaeus wanted to meet Jesus, "He was seeking to see who Jesus was, but on account of the crowd he could not, because he was small in stature" (Luke 19:3, ESV). The crowd was in his way, "so he ran on ahead and climbed up into a sycamore tree" (verse 4). Zacchaeus was determined to turn his needle to *True North*, and because he did so, his eternal destiny was changed. A relationship with Jesus changed his worldview, and with that change came a transformation in the way he viewed his money. Zacchaeus became a Converterlator. His life echoes into eternity because of his encounter with Jesus Christ!

Using the *Crowd* as a reference point always has a catastrophic ending. Following the crowd may feel good temporarily, but the ending is always lasting destruction. We want to avoid this at all costs! "Enter through the narrow gate. For wide is the gate and broad is the road that leads to destruction, and many enter through it" (Matthew 7:13). Following the crowd is easy; following Jesus can sometimes be extremely difficult. We need to set our sights on Jesus and pull away from the crowd.

Finally, we have the *World*, including lures like lust, pride, power, and riches. The problem with the world is the fact that it is in the process of perishing!

> We do, however, speak a message of wisdom among the mature, but not the wisdom of this age or of the rulers of this age, who are coming to nothing.
> —1 Corinthians 2:6

> So we fix our eyes not on what is seen, but on what is unseen, since what is seen is temporary, but what is unseen is eternal.
> —2 Corinthians 4:18

The *World* is doing everything it can to consume our earthly time, talent, and treasure! It is enticing us to invest all of our resources into stuff, activity, and experiences that in the end have no eternal value. For the most part, the world system is held together by force and greed. It caters to developing a self-centered life, a self-first mindset. It is bent on finding life significance in power, fame, status, stuff, and the accumulation of wealth. A wrong emphasis on these things eventually destroys the lives of people and their loved ones who are caught up in them. In many instances the *World* emphasizes striving to get more for doing less. Get as much stuff as you can so you can retire from work and have a life of ease doing what you want to do when you want to do it. The *World* does everything it can to keep us from thinking about the eternal aspect of life.

All the "stuff" of this world, including power and prestige, has the potential to become idols in our lives. When they replace the position that God should have in our hearts, we miss out on the best that God has for us. "Those who cling to worthless idols forfeit the grace that could be theirs" (Jonah 2:8, NIV84).

Unfortunately, for most people the reference points they use to direct their lives are *Self,* the *Crowd,* and the *World*. But we must always remember, none of these are reliable and not one of them will lead to fulfillment! They are all intrinsically flawed because they all keep us from focusing on Jesus Christ.

Even the Christian has to be conscientious about pointing his needle toward Jesus! We can be using the Compass of Life, but if we hold it too close to *Self,* the *Crowd*, or the *World*, the magnetic pull of wrong directions will point us to the wrong road. All three of these false reference points must be kept at a proper distance from us so we get the right readings on our Compass of Life and stay headed in the right direction.

When we direct our mind (the needle) to focus on Jesus (*True North*) we see the heavenly realm revealed to us. It takes discipline and intentionality to focus on Jesus. If we allow our mind to drift away from *True North* by the gravitational pull of *Self,* the *Crowd,* or the *World*, we will lose our way in the spider web of the consumerlator. These influences are like the rifle barrel that was too close to my compass. It nearly sent me to a disastrous end.

SPIRITUAL GPS

The Christian who is actively cultivating his relationship with God has access to a part of the Compass of Life system I like to call the Spiritual Global Positioning System. This *Spiritual GPS* guides us like the GPS system of the world. We have already seen in Scripture that God will direct our steps when we have a right relationship with him. The psalmist made this great discovery also, "I will instruct you and teach you in the way you should go; I will counsel you with my loving eye on you" (Psalm 32:8). With the smart phones of today, we have access to an eye in the sky or a satellite system that knows where we are and that can guide us step by step to a particular destination. The same is true for the Spiritual GPS system. God knows where we are and directs each one of us day by day precisely to where we need to go.

> **When we focus on Jesus we are able to convert the perishables of this world into imperishable treasure for eternity.**

Applying the Compass of Life concept to our lives enables us to become active Converterlators. When we focus on Jesus (*True North*), we are able to ignore *Self*, the *Crowd*, and the *World*, all of which promote our consumerlator tendencies. With our mind pointing to Jesus we are able to convert the perishables of this world into imperishable treasure for eternity.

Pointing Your Life in the Right Direction:

Honestly answer these questions:

- In which direction does the needle of my life *most often* point: True North, Self, Crowd, World? Why does the needle of my life go in

this direction?
- When my life is not directed to Jesus, what factors contribute to me being pulled in the wrong direction? How can I counter these factors?
- How is my converterlating compromised when I am pulled in the wrong direction?
- What steps do I need to take in order for the needle on my Compass of Life to consistently point True North? (Be specific!)
- How can I incorporate more Bible reading and study into my life in order to keep the needle of my life pointing to Jesus?

PART 2
TRANSFORMATION

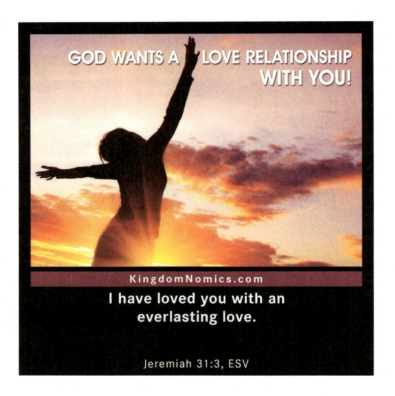

5

Your Relationship with God

Love the Lord your God with all your heart and with all your soul and with all your strength and with all your mind, and your neighbor as yourself.
—Luke 10:27, ESV

Have you ever noticed that when relationships are right, great things can happen? I've even heard it said more than once that who you know is more important than what you know. The all-important relationship; it can either make you or break you, because it is often true that if you have the right connections, certain people can facilitate your way on the upward path of success. People can open doors of opportunity or remove obstacles blocking your way.

Our relationship with God works in much the same way. The Bible tells us that life in this world and the world to come is all about having a growing *relationship* with almighty God. We are not talking here about a relationship of convenience or superficiality; God wants an intimate relationship with us! Jesus Christ came into the world to give us that relationship with God, and our decision to accept salvation through Christ has major implications for not only eternity, but for the time we have remaining in this world.

Being a Converterlator is all about having a right relationship with Jesus Christ and having his Word and life personally operating in your life (see appendix B on page 205). This is a tremendously exciting place to be! When we have a growing *relationship* with God, we experience his favor and blessing. And if we have the favor and blessing of God, what else could we ever need? To have his presence and the truth of his Word operating in our lives through Christ living his life in us truly makes us a different people.

> **God wants an intimate relationship with each one of us!**

Moses modeled this principle for us. The living presence of God in his life was paramount. In fact he did not want to proceed with the tasks God had for him without having God's very presence in his life. "And he said to him, 'If your presence will not go with me, do not bring us up from here'" (Exodus 33:15, ESV).

This kind of *dependence* on God is not possible without *knowing* God and *understanding* how he thinks. This means we must not only *begin* a relationship with him, but go on to *develop* an intimate relationship with him in order to truly *experience* his presence in our lives. Moses realized that if he ever hoped to find favor in God's sight, he needed to know God in a deeper way when he said, "Now therefore, if I have found favor in your sight, please show me now your ways, that I may know you in order to find favor in your sight" (Exodus 33:13, ESV).

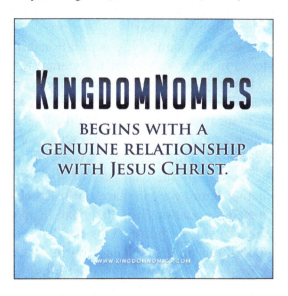

WANTING TO SPEND TIME WITH GOD

What we are talking about here is developing an *intimacy* with God the Father, Jesus Christ, and the Holy Spirit. *Relationship* is not about external rules or a list of what to do and not to do. *Relationship* is about *being with* someone. When we like to be around a person, we make time to be with them. We like to experience their presence for increasing time periods. Each one of us needs to be spending time with God!

My wife, Ruth Ann, and I love each other. We love to spend time together, enjoying each other's company. It doesn't matter what we are doing. There can be long periods of silence, or lots of activity with others. We love to spend time together. We are still learning things about each other even after more than forty-four years of marriage. It is an exciting adventure of "doing life" together!

Moses had this same type of relationship with God. Moses made it very clear he wanted to know God and his ways, and God showed Moses who he really was: "He revealed his character to Moses and his deeds to the people of Israel" (Psalm 103:7, NLT).

People get to know our character when we spend time with them. Actions become somewhat predictable when we know the character of someone. We learn whether or not we can place our trust in them.

The marriage relationship is like that. In marriage, we *learn* to trust our spouse. This is what God did with the children of Israel. They *learned* that God could be trusted. God is always there for us.

My precious granddaughter Sophia loves to come into my study to sit on my lap to play on the keyboard of my computer. After being in my lap for a few minutes one day, I explained to her that I needed to do some work. She understood, left my presence, and I closed the door to my study.

After a few minutes, I heard the pitter patter of little feet running up to my study door. I heard a knocking, and a little loud voice crying, "PaPa, PaPa, I need you!" What do you think I did at that moment? You better believe it. I dropped what I was doing immediately, opened the door, and lifted little Sophia up to my lap to cuddle her.

This is relationship. There is a special bond beyond human description that we have for those who are close and dear to us. As our relationship develops with God, we find we want to spend more and more time with him. He becomes more and more real in our life. We realize his Word literally gives life to our mortal bodies, and he reveals more and more of himself to us. We begin to see his working in the circumstances in our life. We find more and more that we really do need him. Yes, this is the relationship of relationships!

The relationship we develop with God is more precious, more rewarding, more fulfilling than anything else we can see and touch. Abram found this to be the case, "After these things the word of the

Lord came to Abram in a vision, saying, 'Do not be afraid, Abram. I am your shield, your exceedingly great reward'" (Genesis 15:1, NKJV). In the book of Job it is even more specifically stated when it says, "Yes, the Almighty will be your gold and your precious silver" (Job 22:25, NKJV).

Everything boils down to our relationship with God. If we want the *power* of God working in our life, then God must be the God of all things in our life. Every breath and every heartbeat is sourced in God. He is the one who lifts one up and puts another down. He is the one who opens the doors of opportunity.

God responds to the one who has this heart's desire to know him and to the faith of the person who wants his presence in their life. "And [God] said, 'My presence will go with you'" (Exodus 33:14, ESV).

These are the people God is looking for in this world; people who make him the number one priority in their lives. They realize knowing God is central to living successfully in this world. They want to have God's favor on their life. In order for this to happen they need to know his ways so they can follow him. What are you currently doing to keep God number one in your life?

Again, Moses showed us the necessity of having this relationship operating in our lives. "For how shall it be known that I have found favor in your sight, I and your people? Is it not in your going with us, so that we are distinct, I and your people, from every other people on the face of the earth?" (Exodus 33:16, ESV). Our relationship with Christ differentiates us from other people of the world. If we do not have a living and vital relationship with God through Christ, then we are just the same as any other person in the world. When we trust in God, he works in our lives!

There are many things that can keep us from having an intimate relationship with God: other people, confused priorities, "stuff," busyness, you name it! The Converterlator is willing to swim upstream against the world system. We have a different worldview. We live differently, act differently, and are motivated by factors unknown to most of the world. We want God to say to us what he said to Moses, "This very thing that you have spoken I will do, for you have found favor in my sight, and I know you by name" (Exodus 33:17, ESV).

God led Moses and the people through the wilderness of their day. That wilderness was bewildering at times, complex at others, downright confusing, and often threatening! And yet, Moses and the Israelites saw the finger of God at work in their circumstances in numerous ways. When we look to God for direction, we find him to be faithful. We experience him knowing our names, and then we see his hand at work in our daily lives. This creates an incredible sense of expectation as we begin each day. There is nothing more exciting than experiencing Christ living his life through us. We live each day in the relationship we have with him. Cultivating this relationship connects us to the true source of life and power.

> **Cultivating our relationship with God connects us to the true source of life and power.**

GOD AT WORK!

Each one of us wants to experience God in a powerful way. The prophet Isaiah wrote, "That they may see and know, may consider and understand together, that the hand of the Lord has done this, the Holy One of Israel has created it" (Isaiah 41:20, ESV). As we live each day in relationship with God, we see and understand the "God things" that occur in our lives.

This is not to say that life will be easy. There *will* be hard times, but God will be there with us. In my first book, *KingdomNomics,* I recounted how I experienced the Lord lifting a spirit of oppression from me. I have also experienced his presence as I lived through some very difficult situations. He *does* work in our circumstances.

The Bible gives us a wonderful summary about how important our relationship with God is for our time in this world, and how to achieve it: "Now *acquaint* yourself with Him, and be at peace; thereby good will come to you. Receive, please, instruction from His mouth, and lay up His words in your heart" (Job 22:21–22, NKJV, emphasis added). The International Standard Version of the Bible actually words verse 21 this way, "Get to know God, and you'll be at peace with him, and then prosperity will come to you."

Acquainting ourselves with God, or "getting to know him," is the key. The avenues for bringing this about are receiving instruction from his mouth and storing up his Word in our hearts. By discovering the benefits of a living and vital relationship with God through Christ, our value system develops, and we discover the road map for our life. We discover that our relationship with God is more valuable than anything else. Our relationship with God is so important that gold and silver from a value standpoint compared are like the dust of the ground, "Then you will lay your gold in the dust, and the gold of Ophir among the stones of the brooks" (Job 22:24, NKJV). Gold and silver represent the world system's epitome for the ultimate "store of value." In comparison to a living and vital relationship with almighty God they are the equivalent of dust. We must be in God's Word on a regular basis to learn more about him!

Gold and silver are false saviors. Worldly wealth of any kind is a false savior. Only a relationship with God through Christ can deliver. The wise person of today will acquaint himself with God, and become a Converterlator, living to convert the perishable into the imperishable, holding on to values that will echo into eternity. In this case, it really *is* Who you know that counts.

Developing Your Relationship with God:

Take some time to think about, answer, and act on these questions:

- If I am honest, is my relationship with God my number one priority or is it just a relationship of convenience? What things in my life are more important to me than God?

- How much time do I really spend intentionally with God, each day and each week, in worship, Bible reading, and prayer?
- What is currently keeping me from having an intimate relationship with God: other people, confused priorities, "stuff," busyness, something else?
- Do I really believe that my relationship with God can make a difference in my life and in the world? If so, how am I seeing this played out in my life? If not, what do I need to do to have a conviction about this truth?
- What am I currently doing to develop or grow in my relationship with God? What resources are available to me to help me grow in my relationship with God? What step do I need to take to take advantage of these resources?
- Memorize this verse:
"Love the Lord your God with all your heart and with all your soul and with all your strength and with all your mind, and your neighbor as yourself." (Luke 10:27, ESV)

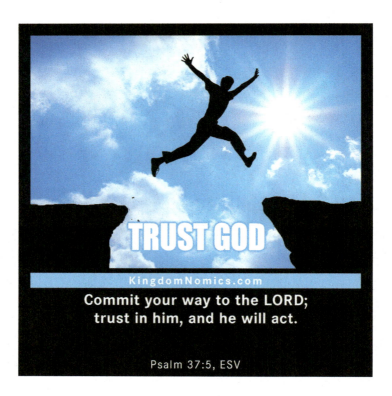

6

Trusting God in All Things

Not that we are sufficient of ourselves to think of anything as being from ourselves, but our sufficiency is from God.
—2 Corinthians 3:5, NKJV

Think about the word *trust* with me for a moment. What does it really mean? *What* do you trust in? *Who* do you trust? And what does your behavior show about your trust—in people and in things? A quick Google search turns up this definition of trust: "assured reliance on the character, ability, strength, or truth of someone or something; one in which confidence is placed." Hmm ... does that describe *your* trust *in God*? Do you have an *assured reliance* in his character, his ability, his strength? Do you have *confidence* in him? It's something to think about, isn't it?

When we accept the salvation of Jesus Christ, it is the first step in becoming the kind of Converterlator

God wants us to be. We begin a journey where life takes on a whole new perspective as we learn what the Bible has to tell us about God and his plan for our lives. Our view of life and our view of this world begin to change as the Spirit of God enlightens us through his Word about this temporary, perishing world and eternity to come. As a result, our goals and motivation for living totally change.

We live in a world where so much is really beyond our control. Variables beyond count impact our lives in ways we would not think possible. If we are to maintain a sense of balance, contentment, and peace in our lives, we must learn to trust in God and his provision for us. This is not an easy concept to grasp, and sometimes it is even more difficult to see "trusting in God" actually working in our lives as we meet the challenges of everyday living. But he *is* there, guiding and directing our lives. The Bible tells us, "Now faith is confidence in what we hope for and assurance about what we do not see" (Hebrews 11:1). We have *confidence* and *assurance* that we can trust in him!

> **We must learn to trust in God and his provision for us.**

The decision to believe in the person of Jesus Christ, alone, for personal salvation is by far the most important life-impacting decision a person will ever make. But our decision to *believe* is only the *beginning*. As we learn more about God, we learn to trust him more, to have confidence in his character, to rely on his ability and strength.

Trusting in God is the most important decision I ever made. However, another very important decision I made was to marry my lovely wife, Ruth Ann. We had a unique encounter and a rather short dating relationship before we decided, based on our faith and trust in God, to marry and become one under the Lordship of Jesus Christ.

Under the best of conditions, marriage is a risk enterprise based on a faith relationship with each other. Both of us were on the staff of a major Christian organization with substantial training and exposure to the Word of God. This gave us great insight into God's plan for marriage, and the roles of the husband and wife. We were on the "same page" when it came to our belief system, and we had a good understanding of what it meant to have a "living relationship" with Christ, both personally and as a couple.

Our "courtship" involved at most three weeks of seeing each other over a period of several months. After I proposed, and she said yes, we had about five months to make the necessary arrangements for our wedding. Since our ministry responsibilities required us to live in different parts of the country, we did not see each other until the date of the wedding, communicating by way of snail mail, packages, and land-line telephone (which was expensive!). We had faith that we were meant to be together.

In the meantime, I met with the ministry's staff psychologist who reviewed the tests we had taken when we joined the staff, and his assessment of our relationship was, "This marriage was made in heaven." We met one of his long-term assistants about two years later and told her this story, and she said, "You folks have to be a one-in-a-million couple; he never says that to anybody." We both just looked at each other and said, "Wow!" But the bottom line was, we still didn't know each other that well!

Let's face it. Each one of us continues to *develop* as an individual after we marry. And relationships continue to grow and change throughout marriage. Before we say "I do" there is a lot we do not know about the other person. We even do not know how we will change over the years. How we respond and react is constantly changing with the factors that impact us along the way.

Ruth Ann and I both had to trust that God was leading us into this most important relationship. We both had a living relationship with God, giving us the confidence this was the right step, the right person, and the right time to make this vital life-changing commitment to our God-given soul mate for life. Marriage for us was truly a "leap of faith" learning to trust in the guidance given to us by God. The years have proven that our trust in God has allowed us to enjoy blessing beyond measure. We've changed and grown, and our trust in God has grown deeper and stronger and we've also learned to trust each other more.

TRUST GROWS

Our relationship with God and the trust we have in him also changes and grows. We use whatever knowledge we have at the time to take a step of faith in establishing a relationship with God. We then embark on a process and a journey that takes place in the heart of every believer for both this world and the world to come. "Salvation" is not the end, but a beginning.

There is more to salvation than just finding the fire escape from this perishing world to a place in heaven someday. It takes *time* for us to be transformed by the renewing of our mind.

> **It takes time for us to grow in our faith and trust in God.**

"The earth produces by itself, first the blade, then the ear, then the full grain in the ear" (Mark 4:28, ESV). Just as it takes time for a crop to grow, it takes time for us to grow in our faith and trust in God.

Salvation is all about saving us from the perishing and preparing us for the imperishable world of eternity to come. The Bible tells us, "So we fix our eyes not on what is seen, but on what is unseen, since what is seen is temporary, but what is unseen is eternal" (2 Corinthians 4:18). After establishing a relationship with Christ by trusting in him alone for our salvation, we find this is just the beginning of a new life process he wants to work out in us, changing everything from our worldview, motivation for living, our goals in life, and our focus ... to preparation for eternity.

TRUST IN ACTION

We exercise our trust every day: in the news reporter, in the engineer who worked on our mode of transportation, in the places where we purchase our food. We make our decisions based on an intrinsic belief that things and people are trustworthy.

Here is a real-life example. In today's world tall buildings have elevators. We enter the building planning to meet someone on the thirtieth floor. To reach that floor we need to enter an elevator, push a button, and wait while a power surge propels the elevator upward to the thirtieth floor. Think for a moment what this process involves. We believe the elevator has the capacity to lift us to the thirtieth floor, and that it will not crash downward. We step on by an act of our will. We have faith, trust, confidence, and conviction that it will work. When we push the button, we trust that the elevator is wired into a source of power that will propel it upward. We now enjoy the benefit of what it is supposed to do.

When it comes to our living relationship with Christ, we engage the same steps. By an act of our will, we push the button of faith, "Commit your way to the Lord; trust in him, and he will act" (Psalm 37:5, ESV). We walk through life, with an expectation of seeing God perform his good work toward us, for our expectation is from him, "My soul, wait silently for God alone, for my expectation is from Him" (Psalm 62:5, NKJV). We have confidence in his promises to work in our lives.

CONVICTION

Conviction is a key component of faith. When a person lacks conviction, their faith wavers and the promises of God may not be fulfilled. Scripture tells us, "When you ask, you must believe and not doubt, because the one who doubts is like a wave of the sea, blown and tossed by the wind. That person should not expect to receive anything from the Lord" (James 1:6–7). Abraham is a prime example of one who was fully persuaded that God would perform what he had promised. That is conviction. Conviction was a controlling factor in Abraham's life, and he ordered his life accordingly, experiencing the blessings of God. "Yet he did not waver through unbelief regarding the promise of God, but was strengthened in his faith and gave glory to God, being fully persuaded that God had power to do what he had promised" (Romans 4:20–21).

We find in the Bible many examples of God working through people who trusted him. Noah pleased God and walked with him. Because of this he was used to save a remnant of the human race and the animals of God's creation from the flood. He was a type of Converterlator, saving the perishing from the onslaught of destruction coming on the earth. Joseph was another person through whom God worked mightily. Through all of his harsh experiences, his trust was in God and the difficulty of life only made him better instead of him becoming bitter. He eventually was elevated to being second in power only to Pharaoh in Egypt. God used him to save his family from famine and provide a place of safety for the Hebrew people.

Moses became an agent of change and deliverance for the people held captive in Egypt. God used all of Moses' experiences to work in and through him to transform him into the leader God needed him to be. We see many others throughout the Bible who were used in a mighty way by God including Joshua, Caleb, Gideon, David, Daniel, Ezra, and Nehemiah. All of them were Converterlators, examples for us to follow in our relationship with God. Besides having faith, all of these people had a desire to live for God. When they knew what the mission was, they, by an act of their will chose to follow God's will.

> **We must have *conviction* that the Word of God is living and powerful and that it works in those who receive and trust in it.**

We must have the conviction that the Word of God is living and powerful and that it works in those who receive and trust in it. The promises of God are all sourced in him and find their "yes" in Jesus Christ. We must have the conviction that we serve a God who sees and provides. When he gives us an assignment, we can be confident of experiencing his provision. "The one who calls you is faithful, and he will do it" (1 Thessalonians 5:24).

TRUSTING GOD AS WE CONVERTERLATE

There are many potential Converterlators sitting on the sidelines. Many times we hear people say, "I know that," or "I've already heard that." Their problem is that they have a "head knowledge" of God, but the relationship has yet to make a difference personally in their lives. They may even have a strong intellectual belief in what the Bible says, but it is not governing their everyday decisions and activities. So what is the problem? How do we get *potential* Converterlators to become *actual* Converterlators?

This is a major problem in the church today. Many Christians only have a head knowledge of Scripture.

They have not truly *accepted* the truth of God's Word with *faith*. Without faith the message does the hearer no good. Faith includes an intellectual acceptance of the truth, plus conviction and confidence that will compel a person to take action. It involves *trust* that God is faithful!

Think of it this way. I can *read* all about Aspirin. I can *study* all about its ingredients and even *memorize* them. However, until I have the conviction and the confidence it will work, motivating me to take that bottle off the shelf, unscrew the cap, and swallow the Aspirin, it will do me no personal good. The same is true of our relationship with God. We can read about him in the Bible, we can memorize verses about him and his mighty deeds. But until we actually *do* something with the information that we have and take a step of faith toward having a trust relationship with him, we do not truly experience God.

PARTNERSHIP WITH GOD

There are Christians who think, "I've made my decision for Christ, now it is 'coast time' for me until I go to heaven." Anyone who has this mindset is in for a rude awakening and great disappointment in the world to come. We are to be in partnership with almighty God and each other, "For we are God's fellow workers. You are God's field, God's building" (1 Corinthians 3:9, ESV). We can actually access and experience the divine power and partnership in the work of God through the great and precious promises of his Word. God "has granted to us his precious and very great promises, so that through them [we] may become partakers of the divine nature, having escaped from the corruption that is in the world because of sinful desire" (2 Peter 1:4, ESV).

God is looking for people that he can use in this world, "For the eyes of the Lord run to and fro throughout the whole earth, to give strong support to those whose heart is blameless toward him" (2 Chronicles 16:9, ESV). Our lives must be sourced in Jesus Christ through faith, for it is a walk of faith that produces the fruit that will last, "filled with the fruit of righteousness that comes through Jesus Christ, to the glory and praise of God" (Philippians 1:11, ESV).

Things change when Jesus Christ assumes control of our lives. We become new creations and are transformed into instruments for service to God. We no longer try to earn our way to God through works. We live our lives by the law of faith, and we become ambassadors for him. We grow in our understanding of who God is and learn to trust him more day by day. The love of Christ molds our attitudes, thinking, and behavioral patterns. Jesus Christ progressively gains control over all aspects of our lives. And we in turn, are able to accomplish great things for him; things that will last for all eternity!

Trusting God:

Consider these questions and answer them honestly:

- At this point in my life, *what and/or who* am I trusting in: for stability, for security, for acceptance, for strength?
- *Why* am I trusting in the things I have identified in the previous question?
- What is keeping me from having full confidence in God and his plan for my life?
- What needs to happen in my life in order for me to develop an assured reliance on the character, ability, strength, and truth of God?
- Have I developed a *partnership* with God? What steps can I take to develop a partnership or take my partnership with God to the next level?
- In what ways is my converterlating directly affected by my relationship with God?

7

SOAKING OUR MINDS IN GOD'S WORD

For the word of God is alive and powerful. It is sharper than the sharpest two-edged sword, cutting between soul and spirit, between joint and marrow. It exposes our innermost thoughts and desires.
— Hebrews 4:12, NLT

As *KingdomNomics* thinkers, we want to know God and need to press on to experience him. As surely as we know that the sun will rise tomorrow, we know that God responds to those who pursue him. We want to grow with the growth that comes from him! And as we grow, we see that God is preparing to do something amazing in our lives. He may bring to light a new opportunity, or a new revelation of himself, or even provide a resource that is beyond anything we could ask, think, or imagine. The possibilities are endless.

So, how do we go about experiencing God and growing in our relationship with him? The most important source of our knowledge of God is found in his Word, the Bible. We need to read it, study it, and apply it to our lives. We need to memorize key verses that will help us stay focused on the things God wants us to do in his world. This is a key principle of *KingdomNomics:* our thinking and actions must be grounded firmly in the Word of God. And, as a direct result, our converterlating is influenced by our understanding and application of what we internalize from the Bible.

SOAK, SOW, AND FLOW

One of the ways that I have found to incorporate God's Word into my life is through a process I call *soak, sow, and flow.* This process was introduced in my first book, *KingdomNomics.* We *soak* our minds in the truths of Scripture, which allows us to *sow* them into our circumstances, and have the Holy Spirit *flow* through them.

In order to experience the *soak, sow, and flow* process, we need to memorize and meditate on core verses — what I call "Spiritual M & Ms" — that will guide our thinking on a daily basis. We want to read God's Word, live it, and then let God perform his will through us. The goal here is to have the Word of God personally operating in our everyday lives.

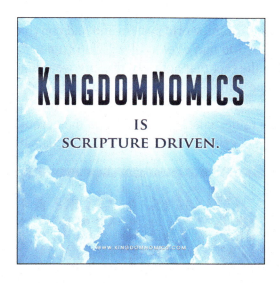

In the Old Testament we read, "I am the Lord your God, who brought you up out of the land of Egypt. *Open your mouth wide, and I will fill it*" (Psalm 81:10, ESV, emphasis added). We want to open our lives up to the truth of God's Word so that he will fill our lives with his goodness. Later in the book of Psalms we read, "How sweet are your words to my taste, sweeter than honey to my mouth!" (Psalm 119:103, ESV). God's Word is wonderfully sweet to our inner being.

GOLD VS. GOD

I want to share with you how my mind was transformed and my attitude toward money was radically changed when I began soaking my heart in the Word of God. From a practical standpoint, material wealth had become the god of my life. The Chief Consumerlator had been extremely successful in deceiving me with the "bling" of the world system and had convinced me that this world had *a lot* to offer! Unfortunately, I was blind to the fact that not only was my wealth going to disappear someday; it was also leading me down the path of destruction. Wealth and material blessings can be like a rattlesnake—deceptive *and* dangerous! And I had been deceived and was on a dangerous path.

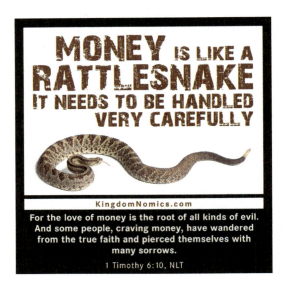

As I became increasingly dissatisfied with my life, one day I took out a piece of paper and wrote the words GOLD and GOD beside each other. We all know that many people make gold or worldly wealth their god and, from a practical standpoint, that is exactly what had happened to me.

As I looked at those two words on my piece of paper, I first placed parentheses around the "L" in GO(L)D. After looking at that for a while, I then blacked out that "L" and had the word GOD! As I sat staring at that word, I was reminded of Jesus' words, "No one can serve two masters. For you will hate one and love the other; you will be devoted to one and despise the other. You cannot serve both God and money" (Matthew 6:24, NLT). As I sat there meditating on that verse, I wrote in an "L" *under* the word GOD. The "L" represented everything I was living for at that time: my money, possessions, opportunities, and time for pleasure. I realized that I needed to place all of these things under the control of God so that he could bring balance into my life for the proper use of these resources. I needed his wisdom to resolve the intrinsic conflicts we all have in determining the balance in managing the perishable and the imperishable. I wanted to increase my focus on participating in the advancement of God's kingdom. This was a huge revelation to me.

At that time I made a basic heart decision, "I am submitting the control of my entire life to the Lord, including anything and everything related to me." That included my time, talent, and treasure. For me, this was a huge undertaking and continues to be a work in progress. Since that time, I have become progressively more of a strategic kingdom investor by investing more of my time, talent, and treasure for the imperishable values of the eternal kingdom. Ruth Ann and I continue to take increasing steps to depositing more of our material wealth in the "Bank of Heaven" for the purpose of advancing the kingdom through endeavors related to the fulfillment of the Great Commission. My motives and talents for generating wealth have been converterlated into making an impact for the kingdom of God. And this has all come about from soaking my heart in the Word of God!

Once we make the discovery that everything we can see and touch is perishable from an eternal perspective, and that we should be focusing our lives on the imperishable values of the kingdom of God, we will have a series of lightbulb moments that will transform our lives.

JUST LIKE A SPONGE

Our mind is like a big, soft sponge. It absorbs everything around it.

How are we transformed into being Converterlators? The Bible tells us, "Do not be conformed to this world, but be transformed by the renewal of your mind, that by testing you may discern what is the will of God, what is good and acceptable and perfect" (Romans 12:2, ESV). The living, powerful Word of God *transforms* our attitudes and our thinking, if we soak our minds in it. This soaking is vital. Our attitudes and convictions, how we think, have a major impact on how we feel and ultimately behave. Here is where the concept of the Spiritual M & Ms comes into play. When we *memorize* and *meditate on* key verses, soaking our minds in them, the transforming power of God's Word changes how we think, feel, and act.

We must have faith that transformation will happen when we do so. Of Abraham the Bible says, "No unbelief made him waver concerning the promise of God, but he grew strong in his faith as he gave glory to God, fully convinced that God was able to do what he had promised" (Romans 4:20–21, ESV). Abraham was fully convinced that God was able to do what he had promised. The question is: *Do* we *have the faith that God's Word will transform and renew* our *minds?*

VERSES TO LIVE BY

It is helpful to have our mind soak on passages of Scripture that describe the power of God in addition to teaching us about his attributes. Many times these passages include why God favors people who pursue his priorities. It is important to reflect on these passages of Scripture because they give us insight into the mind of God and help us to know him better. It takes desire, time, and work to absorb God's Word.

The more we saturate our mind with these truths, the more we will experience transforming power.

Scripture gives us insight into the mind of God and helps us to know him better.

Where to start? Here are some verses that tell us about God. Any one of these (or more!) would be a great place to begin your soaking (memorizing and meditating on) in God's Word.

> The Lord merely spoke, and the heavens were created. He breathed the word, and all the stars were born.
> —Psalm 33:6, NLT

> Ah, Sovereign Lord, you have made the heavens and the earth by your great power and outstretched arm. Nothing is too hard for you.
> —Jeremiah 32:17

> God stretches the northern sky over empty space and hangs the earth on nothing."
> —Job 26:7, NLT

> I am the Lord, the God of all the peoples of the world. Is anything too hard for me?
> —Jeremiah 32:27, NLT

> Let all the earth fear the Lord; let all the inhabitants of the world stand in awe of him! For

he spoke, and it came to be; he commanded, and it stood firm.
—Psalm 33:8–9, ESV

The counsel of the Lord stands forever, the plans of his heart to all generations. Blessed is the nation whose God is the Lord, the people whom he has chosen as his heritage!
—Psalm 33:11–12, ESV

The Lord looks down from heaven and sees the whole human race. From his throne he observes all who live on the earth. He made their hearts, so he understands everything they do.
—Psalm 33:13–15, NLT

Behold, the eye of the Lord is on those who fear him, on those who hope in his steadfast love.
—Psalm 33:18, ESV

Our soul waits for the Lord; he is our help and our shield. For our heart is glad in him, because we trust in his holy name. Let your steadfast love, O Lord, be upon us, even as we hope in you.
—Psalm 33:20–22, ESV

And I am sure of this, that he who began a good work in you will bring it to completion at the day of Jesus Christ.
—Philippians 1:6, ESV

Now then, my children, listen to me; blessed are those who keep my ways. Listen to my instruction and be wise; do not disregard it. Blessed are those who listen to me, watching daily at my doors, waiting at my doorway. For those who find me find life and receive favor from the Lord.

—Proverbs 8:32–35

Call to me and I will answer you and tell you great and unsearchable things you do not know.

—Jeremiah 33:3

Trust in the Lord with all your heart; do not depend on your own understanding. Seek his will in all you do, and he will show you which path to take.

—Proverbs 3:5–6, NLT

And without faith it is impossible to please him, for whoever would draw near to God must believe that he exists and that he rewards those who seek him.

—Hebrews 11:6, ESV

Whoever has my commandments and keeps them, he it is who loves me. And he who loves me will be loved by my Father, and I will love him and manifest myself to him.

—John 14:21, ESV

THE POWER OF GOD'S WORD

When we dig into God's Word, we learn about his indescribable power and greatness. God can create whatever he wants, even out of nothing! God's counsel and his plans stand forever. We can either place ourselves in a position to receive his blessing or not. God's Word is powerful. Active. It accomplishes. Wherever it is sent, it prospers. To fulfill God's purposes, we need to absorb all that is contained in God's Word. As we do so, we learn more about the mind of God and open ourselves to receive his direction. "So is my word that goes out from my mouth: It will not return to me empty, but will accomplish what I desire and achieve the purpose for which I sent it" (Isaiah 55:11). By his Word we are renewed inwardly. His Word is like discovering the treasure of treasures: "For those who find me find life and receive favor from the Lord" (Proverbs 8:35).

"Therefore we do not lose heart. Though outwardly we are wasting away, yet inwardly we are being renewed day by day" (2 Corinthians 4:16). Only the Word of God can renew us and give us true direction. All other pursuits are in vain if they are substitutes for the Word of God in our lives.

The bottom line? There is no way for one to be an effective Converterlator without knowing the Word of God. Along with the Holy Spirit, the Word is the primary means

> **There is no way for us to be effective Converterlators without knowing the Word of God.**

for bringing transformation to our values, attitudes, and mindset. It is also the means for nourishing and fueling the very roots of our being. It is by God's Word that we learn about the will of God and how to implement and execute the plans he reveals to us through his Word.

With our access to technology these days, there are many ways to access God's Word! If you have a Bible, start reading it *today* and select a verse for memorization and meditation. Go online and access a reading program; two that are popular and easily available are through *www.biblegateway.com* and *www.navigators.org*. Many Christian organizations also offer great Bible reading helps through their websites including *www.godresources.org* and *kingdomnomics.com*.

> **When we memorize and meditate on key verses, soaking our minds in them, the transforming power of God's Word changes how we think, feel, and act.**

Unlike other written documents, God's Word is living and powerful. One of my favorite Bible verses is Hebrews 4:12, the verse that opened this chapter: "For the word of God is living and active. Sharper than any double-edged sword, it penetrates even to dividing soul and spirit, joints and marrow; it judges the thoughts and attitudes of the heart" (NIV84). God's Word works in us and through us! Every day, we need to have his Word actively operating in our lives.

Soaking in God's Word:

Take some time to reflect on these questions:

- How consistently do I read and study God's Word? What step do I need to take to make this a more disciplined part of my life?
- How much of God's Word do I have memorized? How can I make this a priority in my life?
- Are there any ways that I can currently see God's Word transforming my life? If not, what step(s) do I need to take to make his Word more operative in my life?
- In what ways would my converterlating become more effective if I were to make the study of God's Word more important in my life?
- Choose to memorize any one of the verses included in this chapter. Meditate on it every day. Pay attention to what God is teaching you through this verse and how he is directing you. After you have lived with this verse for a week or two, move on and memorize another one!

8

SOWING GOD'S WORD

Jesus said ... "I do the will of the One who sent me, finishing the work he started."
—John 4:34, MSG

Recently, my daughter and her family visited our home. One afternoon she requested that I go pick up some pizza for dinner. As I was leaving the house, I stopped to have a conversation with another member of the family. That is when I heard the words, "Stay focused, Daddy! Go get the pizza!"

How often we lose our focus when we are doing God's work! We have good intentions, we begin the journey ... and then we are distracted! We need to stay focused on the important things! Jesus was on a mission. His work was to *do* the will of God and to finish it.

We must stay focused on God's Word and let it influence every situation we encounter.

Each one of us needs this same desire and goal. We must desire to finish the work God has gifted us to do before we leave this world. We are on a mission: a mission to help fulfill the Great Commission, as Jesus commanded in Matthew 28: "Therefore go and make disciples of all nations, baptizing them in the name of the Father and of the Son and of the Holy Spirit, and teaching them to obey everything I have commanded you. And surely I am with you always, to the very end of the age" (Matthew 28: 19–20). The only way that we will accomplish this great task is to stay focused on God's Word and let it influence every situation we encounter.

RECITING SCRIPTURE

Soaking our hearts in the Word of God is really only the first step to making it personally operative in our lives. We need to soak in the words of Scripture *so that* we will have a greater and greater desire to have God's Word influence all areas of our lives, including our converterlating.

After spending a lot of time in the Word, and spending time reflecting on it, I came upon a verse that has become a favorite of mine: "My heart is stirred by a noble theme *as I recite my verses for the king*; my tongue is the pen of a skillful writer" (Psalm 45:1, emphasis added). This verse helped me to develop the concept of *sowing* to the Spirit. The Word of God is living and powerful, and it works in the life of the believer who receives it. Our tongue is the pen of a skillful writer because we are reciting the Word of God *back* to the one who inspired the writing in the first place. The activation process of God's Word actually controlling our behavior is what I refer to as *sowing* to the Spirit.

You may have heard the saying, "You reap what you sow." This idiom means that there is an effect for everything a person does or says, and that the effort a person puts into something will eventually be rewarded appropriately in this life or the next. The general idea behind "you reap what you sow" is that actions have consequences. The effects of a person's behaviors are not necessarily apparent right away, such as when a farmer has to wait a while for a crop to mature; nevertheless, they show up eventually. We sow God's Word out of our hearts and into the world.

As Converterlators our goal is that all of those words would reap eternal benefits!

Sowing to the Spirit of God begins with praising God, rejoicing in his marvelous provision of salvation with expressions of gratitude. God loves and responds to these expressions of faith: "Let the godly sing for joy to the Lord; it is fitting for the pure to praise him. Praise the Lord with melodies on the lyre; make music for him on the ten-stringed harp. Sing a new song of praise to him; play skillfully on the harp, and sing with joy" (Psalm 33:1–3, NLT). "The one who offers thanksgiving as his sacrifice glorifies me; to one who orders his way rightly I will show the salvation of God!" (Psalm 50:23, ESV). What promises to claim for our personal lives! As we recite these verses we are focused on God's power and purposes.

MEDITATION

We often think of meditation as quiet reflection, and it is! But our sowing is directly related to our meditation, because the sowing comes out of the meditation! We see the principle of meditating on God's Word as we read of the birth of Jesus in Luke: "But Mary treasured up all these things and pondered them in her heart" (Luke 2:19). Can you imagine Mary's reaction when the shepherds told her about the supernatural events they experienced when Jesus was born? We learn an important lesson from Mary in this passage. She *treasured up* and *pondered* these things *in her heart*. When we treasure things in our heart, they are special and we think of them often. When we ponder on things that we have been exposed to, we reflect upon their importance and impact. These thoughts help us develop convictions that impact our behavior. Mary's life was forever changed because of this.

The supernatural exposure to God's Word from the angels that the shepherds experienced so impacted them that they were moved to go to Bethlehem to see this miracle for themselves. Their lives were changed and Mary's faith was deepened.

The heart *absorbs* whatever it is soaking in, so a cursory reading of the Bible is not enough. We must *spend time* with God's Word. We must *treasure* its content and *ponder* what it is saying to us. Scripture is living and powerful; it impacts how we think, feel, and act. Again, our sowing *comes from* our meditation. The two are intrinsically linked. Jesus said, "For *out* of the *abundance* of the *heart* the *mouth speaks*" (Matthew 12:34, NKJV, emphasis added).

> **We must *spend time* with God's Word.**

God wants to transform us into the likeness of his Son for service in this world! We will be equipped to make a difference for all eternity when we memorize, ponder, and meditate on his Word. As we spread our wings of faith, the wind of the Spirit lifts our soul above the corrupting influences of the world, cleansing our heart and mind, so we can focus on the kingdom values God wants to instill in the depths of our soul. Reciting our verses and praying them from within our soul, assures that we are praying according to the will of God. And God promises that he hears us and will answer in his way and time. "And this is the boldness we have in God's presence: that if we ask God for anything that agrees with what he wants, he hears us. If we know he hears us every time we ask him, we know we have what we ask from him" (1 John 5:14–15, NCV).

We are counseled in the New Testament to "Let the message of Christ dwell among [us] richly as [we] teach and admonish one another with all wisdom through psalms, hymns, and songs from the Spirit, singing to God with gratitude in [our] hearts" (Colossians 3:16). When we trust in Jesus Christ as our Lord and Savior, we are sealed by the Spirit of God, and we are justified and made acceptable to Almighty God. We are secure in him and are in a position to do the works he has prepared for us to do. When our hearts are filled with his Word, it will help expel the things that would lead us astray, such as wrong attitudes, desires to sin, and the lures of the world. And it will help us to focus on all that he has for us.

PRAYING VERSES BACK TO GOD

I find my own heart is stirred when I recite and pray my Spiritual M & M verses to the King. When we do this we know we are praying in accordance with the will of God. After all, it is his Word we are sowing back to him. And I have found that God responds in a powerful way when I do this. As we pray these verses back to God, we begin to experience what David did in his life:

The Lord is my strength and shield. I trust him with all my heart. He helps me, and my heart is filled with joy. I burst out in songs of thanksgiving.
—Psalm 28:7, NLT

The Lord is my strength and my song; he has become my salvation.
—Psalm 118:14, ESV

The prophet Isaiah also experienced God in a powerful way:

Behold, God is my salvation; I will trust, and will not be afraid; for the Lord G<small>OD</small> is my strength and my song, and he has become my salvation. With joy you will draw water from the wells of salvation.
—Isaiah 12:2–3, ESV

But those who hope in the Lord will renew their strength. They will soar on wings like eagles; they will run and not grow weary, they will walk and not be faint.
—Isaiah 40:31

Jesus tells us his words are life. They shed light within, enlightening our heart, strengthening our inner person, so the person of Jesus Christ can dwell in our heart. The Apostle Paul wrote:

> Let the word of Christ dwell in you richly, teaching and admonishing one another in all wisdom, singing psalms and hymns and spiritual songs, with thankfulness in your hearts to God.
> —Colossians 3:16, ESV

> I pray that out of his glorious riches he may strengthen you with power through his Spirit in your inner being, so that Christ may dwell in your hearts through faith. And I pray that you, being rooted and established in love, may have power, together with all the Lord's holy people, to grasp how wide and long and high and deep is the love of Christ, and to know this love that surpasses knowledge—that you may be filled to the measure of all the fullness of God.
> —Ephesians 3:16–19

In Jeremiah we read, "When your words came, I ate them; they were my joy and my heart's delight, for I bear your name, Lord God Almighty" (Jeremiah 15:16). Here, we see the mechanics for experiencing God in our lives. When the words of God came to him, Jeremiah *ate* them. In other words, he *internalized* them by *memorizing* and *meditating on* them (Spiritual M & Ms!). These words became his heart's delight! That is why I like to say, "Read it, eat it, live it ... and God will visit to perform his Word toward you."

In the book of Psalms we read, "Take delight in the Lord, and he will give you the desires of your heart"

(Psalm 37:4). As we delight in the Lord and his Word, his desires will become our desires. Our prayer life will come into harmony with his will. We will see more answered prayer because we are praying in conformance to his desires: "This is the confidence we have in approaching God: that if we ask anything according to his will, he hears us. And if we know that he hears us—whatever we ask—we know that we have what we asked of him" (1 John 5:14–15).

> **Read it, eat it, live it ... and God will visit to perform his Word toward you.**

The way we think, act, and talk all reflect what is in our hearts. What we nurture in our hearts will govern our behavior. We need to stay focused on God's Word in order to be filled with Christ and accomplish his purposes. When we sow God's Word, we will find that our converterlating takes on new direction, meaning, and impact!

Sowing God's Word:

Carefully think about these questions and apply them to your life:

- Have I ever thought about God's Word influencing my life throughout my day? When have I experienced God's Word directly affecting a situation in my life?
- In what ways can I *immediately* begin sowing God's Word?

- In what ways do I see the meditation of God's Word coming out in my words and actions?
- How can the concept of sowing potentially impact my converterlating?
- Choose one of the verses included in the section "Praying Verses Back to God." Sow this verse every day for one week and pay attention to what you see happening in your life because of it.

9

LETTING THE SPIRIT FLOW

So I say, walk by the Spirit, and you will not gratify the desires of the flesh.
—Galatians 5:16

We *soak*, we *sow*, and then the Spirit *flows*! This is how we experience God's power in our lives. The Holy Spirit works in us and through us to accomplish God's purposes. It is through the Spirit's power that we obtain the wisdom and ability to be Converterlators. When we spend time in God's Word, we experience what I like to call a *flowback* from the Holy Spirit; the Holy Spirit working in us and through us in a variety of ways.

As a child I was taken to an amusement park from time to time and we would always ride on the bumper cars! You know, those cars that had large rubber rings around them to protect the drivers. The fun of this ride was trying to bump the other cars. Sometimes I would get hit really hard, and that would make me want to hit back as hard as possible.

> **The Holy Spirit's power allows us to respond to all of our life circumstances with his strength.**

Life is like this. We are always being "bumped" by circumstances and other people. Sometimes these bumps can be really hard, and our response is to hit back as hard as possible. At those moments we have a decision to make: Will we let the old flesh control us, or will the Holy Spirit control us? In so many ways we are weak, powerless, and vulnerable. However, we have been born to a living hope and we are kept by the power of God. It is the Holy Spirit's power that allows us to respond to all of our life circumstances with his strength.

FLOWING

Many Christians today have *heard* about the Holy Spirit, but they have not *encountered* him in a life-changing way. When we first ask Jesus into our lives, the Holy Spirit flows his life into our mortal bodies. The Spirit's work begins in us when we first receive Christ into our lives: "If the Spirit of him who raised Jesus from the dead dwells in you, he who raised Christ Jesus from the dead will also give life to your mortal bodies through his Spirit who dwells in you" (Romans 8:11, ESV). This sets the stage for us to flow with the Spirit in our everyday lives. It is the Holy Spirit that gives us the power to overcome the sinful impulses of the flesh and the lures of the world that cause us to spend too much time on perishable aspects of this life.

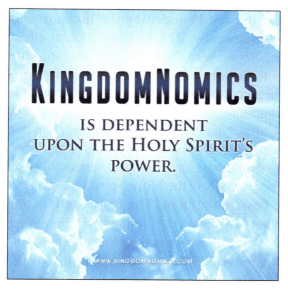

It is because of the work of Jesus Christ on the cross that the Holy Spirit's power flows through us and enables us to be Converterlators. The Bible tells us, "I have been crucified with Christ and I no longer live, but Christ lives in me. The life I now live in the body, I live by faith in the Son of God, who loved me and gave himself for me" (Galatians 2:20). Our responsibility is to get self out of the way so the life of Christ can live and minister through us. We will see the life of Christ flow through us as we allow the Spirit of God to crucify the selfish desires that interfere with his working presence. This is a transforming process done by degrees, "And we all ... are being transformed into the same image from one degree of glory to another. For this comes from the Lord" (2 Corinthians 3:18, ESV).

This concept is so exciting because it takes us into a realm not bounded by the limitations of the world we see now. There is no limit to what God can do! No wonder Paul prayed, "Now to him who is able to do immeasurably more than all we ask or imagine, according to his power that is at work within us" (Ephesians 3:20). This is the resurrection power of Jesus Christ. No perceived earthly power can possibly be compared to this. The prospect of that power operating in us and our circumstances is extremely exciting!

When we allow the Holy Spirit to control us, his power flows through us. The Holy Spirit is the only one who can make the converterlating process a reality in our lives. He is the One who enables us to participate with God to accomplish his work. The Spirit giving life to our mortal body brings inward transformation. Paul made this clear when he said, "Therefore we do not lose heart. Though outwardly we are wasting away, yet inwardly we are being renewed day by day" (2 Corinthians 4:16). Flowing with the Spirit is the supernatural outcome of soaking and sowing to the Spirit. It is the outcome of our relationship with God.

The Holy Spirit releases the life and power of God into our lives.

When a lamp is plugged into a wall socket properly and the switch is turned to "on," there is a dynamic relationship established with the source of electrical power;

properly engaged, the power flows and the lamp lights up giving light. The same is true with our relationship with the Spirit of God. The Holy Spirit is the divine power source, releasing the life and power of God into our lives when we are properly connected to him. There are many times when I spend time in God's Word and the Holy Spirit prompts me to make better business and investment decisions. In fact, he directs my decision making in every area of life and orchestrates truth that impacts my everyday life.

God is always on the move. He is always working. There is a divine dynamic that begins to play in our lives when we soak our hearts in his Word, and when we sow his Word to the Spirit.

SEALS, REVEALS, AND DEALS

All of these truths become a reality in our lives when the Holy Spirit seals, reveals, and deals with us. The Holy Spirit first *seals* us at the point of our spiritual birth, "In him you also, when you heard the word of truth, the gospel of your salvation, and believed in him, were *sealed* with the promised Holy Spirit" (Ephesians 1:13, ESV, emphasis added). In Bible times, a seal was a type of security. It was typically used to guarantee a document or letter, indicate ownership, or protect against tampering. The Holy Spirit is our seal in every sense of this word; we are guaranteed, owned, and protected!

The assurance that we experience because of the Holy Spirit's seal sets us free to be Converterlators in the time we have remaining in this temporary world.

After the Holy Spirit seals us, he begins to *reveal* the things of God to us. In 1 Corinthians 2:10–16 we read:

> These are the things God has revealed to us by his Spirit. The Spirit searches all things, even the deep things of God. For who knows a person's thoughts except their own spirit within them? In the same way no one knows the thoughts of God except the Spirit of God. What we have received is not the spirit of the world, but the Spirit who is from God, so that we may understand what God has freely given us. This is what we speak, not in words taught us by human wisdom but in words taught by the Spirit, explaining spiritual realities with Spirit-taught words. The person without the Spirit does not accept the things that come from the Spirit of God but considers them foolishness, and cannot understand them because they are discerned only through the Spirit. The person with the Spirit makes judgments about all things, but such a person is not subject to merely human judgments, for, 'Who has known the mind of the Lord so as to instruct him?' But we have the mind of Christ.

The Holy Spirit opens our hearts to spiritual truth. This gives us the ability to both understand and respond to God's calling as we converterlate our time, talent, and treasure. Without the Holy Spirit in our lives we will not have the things of God revealed to us.

As the Holy Spirit reveals the things of God to us, he also *deals* with us. Jesus said, "It is the Spirit who gives life" (John 6:63, ESV). We choose to live under his control. It is through the Holy Spirit that God works in us and through us, "For it is God who works in you to will and to act in order to fulfill his good purpose" (Philippians 2:13). It is the Holy Spirit's power that allows us to serve God's purposes in God's way. In the Old Testament the prophet Ezekiel recorded God's promise to us, "And I will put my Spirit in you and move you to follow my decrees and be careful to keep my laws" (Ezekiel 36:27).

EXPERIENCING POWER

When we flow with the Spirit we experience his power as we navigate our way through everyday decisions and experiences: "You will receive power when the Holy Spirit comes on you" (Acts 1:8). It is the Holy Spirit that guides our lives daily: "If we live by the Spirit, let us also keep in step with the Spirit" (Galatians 5:25, ESV). The person who practices *soak, sow, and flow* is an empowered Converterlator, ready to perform their assigned tasks!

When we fail to follow the Holy Spirit's leading, we need to confess our sin and ask the Holy Spirit to again assume control. The Bible tells us, "If we confess our sins, he is faithful and just and will forgive us our sins and purify us from all unrighteousness" (1 John 1:9). Our old selves will constantly seek to reassert themselves, and when they do, we need to run back to God!

As we grow in our relationship with Jesus Christ, the Holy Spirit will reveal more and more to us as we mature and do the things he discloses to us. As the Spirit empowers us, we will find ourselves more responsive to God, presenting ourselves to him for his service. Our relationship with God is all about these truths being worked out in our lives through the various circumstances we encounter. We *learn* to depend on the Holy Spirit's power. And it is at this particular juncture that we experience God's direction in ways we never anticipated! This is what the Bible means when it says, "'No eye has seen, no ear has heard, and no mind has imagined what God has prepared for those who love him.' But it was to us that God revealed these things by his Spirit. For his Spirit searches out everything and shows us God's deep secrets" (1 Corinthians 2:9–10, NLT).

We choose to be controlled by the Spirit. We ask the Spirit to control our mind. We choose to set our mind on things above. By the power of the Spirit we bring our thoughts into captive obedience to Jesus Christ: "So I say, let the Holy Spirit guide your lives. Then you won't be doing what your sinful nature craves" (Galatians 5:16, NLT). This requires active participation on our part by the act of our will choosing moment by moment to be controlled by the Spirit.

If you don't know much about the Holy Spirit, now would be a good time to learn more about him. Go to the websites included in chapter 7 (page 106) and learn more about what the Bible has to say about the Holy Spirit and his active role in your life.

When we invite the Holy Spirit to guide and direct and lead us, he shows up in a big way! He transforms us *and* everything that we do ... including our converterlating! He fills us daily and equips us for service. He gives us joy and excitement and fulfillment. He draws us into a deeper relationship with God. He gives us insight into God's Word. He leads us to victorious living.

LETTING THE HOLY SPIRIT HAVE CONTROL

There is a war inside each of us. Though the old flesh wants to reassert itself, the power of the Spirit can overcome it if we ask in faith for him to control how we think, feel, act, and talk. In Romans 8 we read, "The mind controlled by the Spirit is life and peace" (Romans 8:6, NIV84). The mind is key (remember when we talked about the Compass of Life in chapter 4?). The battle first takes place in our head. The people or the things that control our mind control us. It is crucial for us to allow the Holy Spirit to control us:

> Those who live according to the flesh have their minds set on what the flesh desires; but those who live in accordance with the Spirit have their minds set on what the Spirit desires.
> —Romans 8:5

> Set your minds on things above, not on earthly things.
> —Colossians 3:2, NIV84

> Since we live by the Spirit, let us keep in step with the Spirit.
> —Galatians 5:25

It takes intentionality to live life under the control of the Holy Spirit. Every day I ask the Holy Spirit to guide and direct my interactions and decisions. I am learning he is orchestrating everything that impacts my life. He gives me insights and guidance in my business and investment decisions. I have learned, "But remember the Lord your God, for it is he who gives you the ability to produce wealth, and so confirms his covenant, which he swore to your ancestors, as it is today" (Deuteronomy 8:18).

God is the One who enables us to prosper, "Thus says the Lord, your Redeemer, the Holy One of Israel: 'I am the Lord your God, who teaches you to profit, who leads you in the way you should go'" (Isaiah 48:17, ESV). And it is always God who gives the increase, "I planted, Apollos watered, but God gave the increase. So then neither he who plants is anything, nor he who waters, but God who gives the increase" (1 Corinthians 3:6–7, NKJV).

In the business world, a *general partner* is also commonly a *managing partner*, which means that this person is active in the day-to-day operations of the business. I constantly remember that the Holy Spirit is the general partner of my life. He calls the shots. My job is to cooperate with him in everything I do and in all aspects of my life. Everything I have is sourced in God. The Holy Spirit is orchestrating everything that occurs in my life. It is the Spirit's power that has enabled me to be a Converterlator.

> **It is our job to cooperate with the Holy Spirit in everything we do.**

From a kingdom-impact standpoint, I have learned that being a Converterlator is not simply for those involved specifically in Christian ministry. For a short period of my life, God led me into "full-time ministry" with a large Christian organization. I met my lovely wife, Ruth Ann, there and I learned in depth more about having a living relationship with God. However, in time the Holy Spirit led us from that full-time ministry position into the business world to serve God there. It was in the business world the Lord taught me the concepts and principles that are being shared in this book and other materials. *KingdomNomics* now has a worldwide movement, with a website, a project manager, a team of people helping with materials, and tens of thousands of people being exposed to the life-changing concepts regarding the use of time, talent, and treasure for the purpose of expanding the kingdom of God.

With each passing day, I am seeing the truth of this passage of Scripture, "I will open rivers on the bare heights, and fountains in the midst of the valleys. I will make the wilderness a pool of water, and the dry land springs of water. I will put in the wilderness the cedar, the acacia, the myrtle, and the olive. I will set in the desert the cypress, the plane and the pine together, that they may see and know, may consider and understand together, that the hand of the Lord has done this, the Holy One of Israel has created it" (Isaiah 41:18–20, ESV). The finger of God is responsible for everything that has occurred in my life!

I do my best to avoid the mistake made by the last king of Babylon, Belshazzar, who learned the hard way that God is in charge of everyone's life, no matter what their station. He made the great mistake of idolizing the perishable things of this world, "And you have lifted yourself up against the Lord of heaven ... And you have praised the gods of silver and gold, bronze and iron, wood and stone, which do not see or hear or know; and the God who holds your breath in His hand and owns all your ways, you have not glorified ... You have been weighed in the balances, and found wanting ... Your kingdom has been divided, and given to the Medes and Persians" (Daniel 5:23–28, NKJV). That very night he was murdered.

TOTAL COMMITMENT

If we hope to be effective in practicing the *KingdomNomics* principles, we must experience a continuing and growing relationship with the person of Jesus Christ. This only happens when the Holy Spirit performs his functions within our hearts. It is the Holy Spirit who reveals the things of God to us. Our relationship with God is one of God continually revealing himself to us as we practice the concepts of *soak, sow, and flow*. The Spirit searches all things, including the deep things of God. Therefore, unless the Holy Spirit reveals these things to us, we will never find out about them. Without revelation from the Holy Spirit, we cannot bring our lives into proper conformance to the will of God, and we cannot be effective Converterlators.

God is looking for people who are willing to make a total commitment. He wants each one of us to be devoted to the team. We are talking about eternity here. The eternal destinies of people are at stake. God wants people in his kingdom, and then he wants each person to be a committed team player for the advancement of his kingdom. The effective Converterlator is filled with the Holy Spirit and depends on his power and wisdom to accomplish all that God desires!

Flowing with the Spirit:

Think about these questions:

- If I'm honest, am I a player, or am I just sitting in the stands watching?
- If I am just watching, how can I open myself up to the work of the Holy Spirit to become a player?
- If I am a player, am I being empowered by the Holy Spirit to be effective on the field?
- In what ways have I experienced the *flow* of the Holy Spirit?
- Do I truly understand the work and the role of the Holy Spirit in my life? Do I need to take some time to learn more about what the Bible has to say about the Holy Spirit?
- What areas of my life need to be surrendered to the Holy Spirit? Make a list and ask him to take control of each area and to enable you to live your life fully for God.
- If I allow the Holy Spirit to flow in my life, how might my converterlating be changed, focused, or redirected?

PART 3
CONVERTERLATION

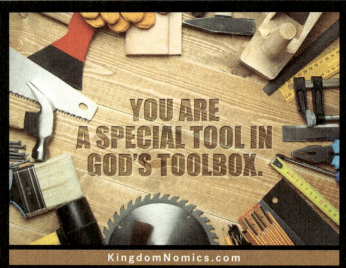

10

YOU'VE BEEN DESIGNED BY GOD FOR A PURPOSE!

"For I know the plans I have for you," declares the Lord.

—Jeremiah 29:11

We all want to make a difference. I have found that most people really want to do something of lasting value and impact. We want to be involved in doing something that will make our lives count. And yes, we often want some kind of recognition and other people's praise for what we do. But it's important to remember that our eternal significance is not found in doing things that others see as important. God wants us to experience *real* significance; and that significance only comes through his unconditional love and total acceptance, and our fulfilling his plan for our lives. Psalm 139:13–16 tells us:

> For you created my inmost being; you knit me together in my mother's womb. I praise you because I am fearfully and wonderfully made; your works are wonderful, I know that full well. My frame was not hidden from you when I was made in the secret place, when I was woven together in the depths of the earth. Your eyes saw my unformed body; all the days ordained for me were written in your book before one of them came to be.

Each one of us has been designed by God for a special purpose! God has fashioned each one of us individually; he created us, formed us, and knows us by name. And he made us to be in a relationship with him. You may be thinking, "Really, has God designed little old me for something special in this world?" There are numerous places in the Bible that confirm that the answer to that question is a definite "Yes!" In the Old Testament we read, "From the place of His dwelling He looks on all the inhabitants of the earth; He fashions their hearts individually; He considers all their works" (Psalm 33:14–15, NKJV).

God is working in *us* to fulfill his purposes, "For it is God who works in you to will and to act in order to fulfill his good purpose" (Philippians 2:13). The Word of God is working in us, "Is not my word like fire, declares the Lord, and like a hammer that breaks the rock in pieces?" (Jeremiah 23:29, ESV). God's Word is like a fire that begins to consume us, burning away the dross of the temporary, refining us, and transforming us into the Converterlators God wants us to be. The Word of God is truly like a hammer, breaking the "rock of self" into pieces, so Christ can shine his life through us to continue his ministry in this world.

A TOOL IN GOD'S TOOLBOX

Our hearts have been individually fashioned by God. Each one of us is special. When you look in a regular toolbox, you find many different kinds of tools, each one designed for a specific purpose. Inside a typical toolbox you may find a hammer, screwdriver, small saw, tape measure, or even a level of some kind. Each tool has a specific purpose. Using them for something other than the purpose they have been designed for usually results in failure. The same is true for us as Christians. Each one of us is a tool in God's toolbox. We have been designed in a specific way for a specific purpose and we need to figure out what that purpose is. First Corinthians 12:4–7 tells us, "There are different kinds of gifts, but the same Spirit distributes them. There are different kinds of service, but the same Lord. There are different kinds of working, but in all of them and in everyone it is the same God at work. Now to each one the manifestation of the Spirit is given for the common good." The Converterlator says, "I want Christ to live and work through me. Here I am, a special person, uniquely

> "I am a special person, uniquely gifted by God!"

gifted by God, designed for a special purpose, and more specifically to do good works that God has created for me to do."

It's important that we understand what each tool is designed to do and then use it in the way it is designed. You can't really evaluate the effectiveness of a tool if you don't know what it is supposed to accomplish. It may look pretty. It may be intriguing. It may look like it has great strength. But you can't judge the excellence of its design until you actually use it.

I experienced this in my own life. I was in God's Toolbox, but I didn't really understand what kind of a tool I was. I had to figure out if I was a hammer, a screwdriver, or a saw. There was no point in trying to be a saw if I had been designed to be a hammer. For me, it took a lot of time. After graduating from college and law school, I entered the business world, and began to experience some success.

After Christ came into my life, I left the secular world and joined the staff of Campus Crusade for Christ. Even though I was serving the Lord in full-time ministry, I sensed, after a few years, I could have a greater impact for the expansion of the kingdom of God in the business world because of my particular gifts, talents, and interests.

Therefore, I left my full-time ministry position and returned to the business world to focus on business investments. I came to the conclusion that I was designed to serve the Lord in the secular world. This was my calling. *This* was my "full-time ministry" for God.

As I have served the Lord in this way, he has allowed me to "road test" the *KingdomNomics* concepts. He then prompted me to write my first book, *KingdomNomics*, with a focus on communicating how the Word of God can become personally operative in our lives, transforming us into becoming strategic kingdom investors. This led to founding the *KingdomNomics* worldwide ministry. It is a journey for many of us as we utilize our gifts, abilities, and opportunities along the way. We experience God's best for us and have the most significance when we move in faith to find God's purposes for using the talents he has given us.

Even though we may think our time, talent, and/or treasure is small or insignificant, God can take them and exponentially multiply them for the advancement of his kingdom. We learn a tremendous *KingdomNomics* principle from the small boy in the New Testament who gave his two small fish and five barley loaves of bread to Jesus. "Here is a boy with five small barley loaves and two small fish, but how far will they go among so many?" (John 6:9). The disciple Andrew questions how so little can be relevant when they were trying to figure out how to feed a *multitude* of people. But Jesus took that little boy's offering, which was insignificant in the eyes of the world, and miraculously used it to feed 5,000 people!

> **No matter what kind of tool we are, we need to be available to God!**

Each one of us needs to be a "five loaves and two fish" person, willing to share so Jesus can do great things through us when we make ourselves available to him. This little boy's life echoes through eternity because he was willing to share what he had and yield himself to the purposes of God. No matter what kind of tool we are, we need to be available to God! God created us and has given us life. He orchestrates all that we do and we need to cooperate with him in every way.

GOD'S PURPOSES

It is critical to understand that what we are talking about here is a work that is being done by God, and not by us. The Bible tells us:

> We now have this light shining in our hearts, but we ourselves are like fragile clay jars containing this great treasure. This makes it clear that our great power is from God, not from ourselves.
> —2 Corinthians 4:7, NLT

God is always on the move in the ever changing circumstances of this world. He is also at work in each one of us.

The apostle Paul wrote, "He [Jesus] gave his life to free us from every kind of sin, to cleanse us, and to make us his very own people, totally committed to doing good deeds" (Titus 2:14, NLT). God has created us, designed us, *and* given us various capacities for doing the good works that he has prepared for us to do. It is a contradiction in terms to be a Converterlator and not be out there as an agent of change.

For me personally, when I think of what salvation has accomplished, I am *compelled* to be a Converterlator, actively doing whatever I can do to help advance the kingdom of God. Think about these two passages of Scripture:

> Giving thanks to the Father, who has qualified you to share in the inheritance of the saints in light. He has delivered us from the domain of darkness and transferred us to the kingdom of his beloved Son, in whom we have redemption, the forgiveness of sins.
> —Colossians 1:12–14, ESV

> Truly, truly, I say to you, whoever hears my word and believes him who sent me has eternal life. He does not come into judgment, but has passed from death to life.
> —John 5:24, ESV

Wow! God has *qualified* us to share in *all* of the benefits of having a *relationship* with him both now and forever. As I understand what all of that means, I really get excited about what God has done, and what he is doing. God has also *delivered* us from the domain of darkness, the hopeless state or condition of our sin that held us captive under the dominion of the Chief Consumerlator. God has *freed* us from that awful state, and *transferred* us to the kingdom of his

Son, granting us access to the transforming promises of God. We have already passed from death to life! We are freed now so that we can be Converterlators, changing the eternal destinies of people, building treasure in heaven, and leveraging time, talent, and treasure for the imperishable values of heaven.

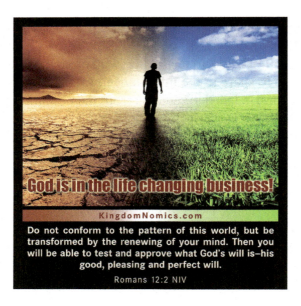

As we seek to accomplish God's purposes, it is important to stay focused on God's plans. As we converterlate our resources we need to be careful not to play to the applause of the world. It is easy to be swayed by the praise of those around us, even as we seek to do God's will. The temptation is always out there to be involved in the more visible types of spiritual endeavors, such as making an effort to be in more prominent positions of leadership, or giving our money in places where our donations will be publicly recognized. However, we must stay focused on God's ultimate plans and desires.

One of my goals as a practitioner of *KingdomNomics* is to be a low-profile, high-impact Converterlator for helping to fulfill the Great Commission. I want to have a low profile so as to not draw unnecessary attention, but I want to be making a big impact! Think about the soccer team or the football team. Each player is most significant when they are fulfilling the role they were designed for. In order to win, each player must play in the position he has been assigned. You are the most significant and have the most impact when you are faithfully filling the position on the team where the coach has placed you.

GOD TRULY IS AT WORK IN OUR LIVES!

As we grow in our relationship with God we will find ourselves becoming increasingly more Christ-centered. As we become more Christ-centered, we will focus more on the will of God. "You won't spend the rest of your lives chasing your own desires, but you will be anxious to do the will of God" (1 Peter 4:2, NLT). And as we focus on God's will, we will increasingly experience his grace: "And God is able to make all grace abound to you, so that having all sufficiency in all things at all times, you may abound in every good work" (2 Corinthians 9:8, ESV).

God working in the lives of his people is a huge theme in the Scripture. "From of old no one has heard or perceived by the ear, no eye has seen a God besides you, who acts for those who wait for him. You meet him who joyfully works righteousness, those who remember you in your ways" (Isaiah 64:4–5, ESV). He acts for those who wait for him!

"For the eyes of the Lord run to and fro throughout the whole earth, to give strong support to those whose heart is blameless toward him" (2 Chronicles 16:9, ESV). God is actually searching for people he can strongly support here in this world! I want to make sure my heart is blameless before God. I want to make sure my heart is completely his. I want to be a person God can strongly support!

All we have to do is meet God's conditions, "Commit to the Lord whatever you do, and he will establish your plans" (Proverbs 16:3). When we commit our way to him, having the expectation that he will act, we can have confidence that God will respond to us in his way and time. Moses got it right, "Now therefore, if I have found favor in your sight, please show me now your ways, that I may know you in order to find favor in your sight. Consider too that this nation is your people" (Exodus 33:13, ESV). And in response, "He [God] made known his ways to Moses, his acts to the people of Israel" (Psalm 103:7, ESV).

> **God has designed us for a purpose and he will provide his presence and strength to help us accomplish that purpose.**

Moses experienced the favor of God, and both he and the people witnessed God working in their lives and circumstances. I strongly believe having the favor of God on one's life should be our paramount desire. When Christ shines on our life, things happen. In Proverbs it says, "For whoever finds me finds life and obtains favor from the Lord" (Proverbs 8:35, ESV). When we have the favor of God, we have everything we need. God has designed us for a purpose and he will provide his presence and strength to help us accomplish that purpose. The Bible encourages us with these words: "'I will never leave you nor forsake you.' So we can confidently say, 'The Lord is my helper; I will not fear; what can man do to me?'" (Hebrews 13:5–6, ESV). When we have a relationship with God through Jesus Christ, he is with us!

POWER FOR EACH DAY

Whatever we are facing, God is with us! "So do not fear, for I am with you; do not be dismayed, for I am your God. I will strengthen you and help you; I will uphold you with my righteous right hand" (Isaiah 41:10). Remember, we have the resurrection power of Christ in us. God is working inside of us for the purpose of enabling us to do his will. John reminds us of this very truth when he writes, "You, dear children, are from God and have overcome them, because the one who is in you is greater than the one who is in the world" (1 John 4:4). Satan will try to convince us that our lives don't matter. We need to take a stand against that kind of thinking. Jesus is our salvation and strength. We need to be looking to him and expecting to see his hand at work in our lives. The prophet Jeremiah wrote, "'For I am with you,' declares the Lord, 'to deliver you'" (Jeremiah 1:19, ESV). When we allow God's power to work through us, we are not only significant; we can accomplish significant things for God's kingdom.

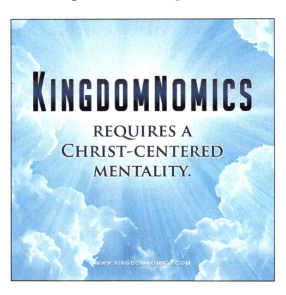

Each one of us needs to answer the question: *What is God's purpose for me?* Once we have the answer to that question, we need to figure out *how* we can successfully fulfill that purpose. After all, each one of us will stand before the Judgment Seat of Christ someday to render an accounting. There is no way to avoid that appointment. That is a sobering thought to me; what I do matters, and it actually matters to others as well. I want to be about my Father's business! I want to soak my heart in the Word of God, feed my soul with Spiritual M & Ms, and let the Spirit flow through me. I want God to reveal his plan and purpose for my life to me so that his desires become my desires. I want him to do his work in me and through me. I want to be a Converterlator! "Now to him who is able to do far more abundantly than all that we ask or think, according to the power at work within us, to him be glory in the church and in Christ Jesus throughout all generations, forever and ever. Amen" (Ephesians 3:20–21, ESV).

ETERNAL SIGNIFICANCE

With the passing of time, the significance of what we have done will be revealed. Will we have used our resources for the perishable or imperishable? We can do things that others value. We can have an impact on their lives by meeting urgent needs. We can affect people's lives for a long time. We can even receive praise and applause for what we do. Ultimately, however, the impact of what we have done will be revealed in eternity: "Everyone's work will be put through the fire so that all can see whether or not it keeps its value, and what was really accomplished. Then every workman who has built on the foundation with the right materials, and whose work still stands, will get his pay. But if the house he has built burns up, he will have a great loss" (1 Corinthians 3:13–15, TLB).

Only God can give us true significance. We have individual significance because we belong to him and he has created us to do a special work for him. Are you embracing the specific responsibilities that he has given you? There are things we will not know or even understand until eternity, but we do know this:

"I chose you and appointed you so that you might go and bear fruit–fruit that will last" (John 15:16). Don't settle for an illusion of significance. Stake your self-worth on the promises of God's Word.

Staying True to Your Purpose:

Take some time to consider these questions:

- In what ways do I see God working in my life?
- What kind of tool am I in God's toolbox? What specific talents or abilities do I have? How am I using my abilities to converterlate my resources?
- If I'm honest, are there things that I am converterlating in order that I might receive the applause of the world?
- What am I doing to stay focused on what God wants *me* to be accomplishing?
- As a Converterlator, what am I currently doing that is low profile? What am I doing that is high profile? Is my focus in the right place?
- Is my converterlating high impact or low impact? What needs to change in my approach?
- At this point in my life, *what* is God's purpose for me and *how* am I fulfilling that purpose?

11

CONVERTERLATING YOUR TIME

And now I have a word for you who brashly announce, "Today—at the latest, tomorrow—we're off to such and such a city for the year. We're going to start a business and make a lot of money." You don't know the first thing about tomorrow. You're nothing but a wisp of fog, catching a brief bit of sun before disappearing. Instead, make it a habit to say, "If the Master wills it and we're still alive, we'll do this or that."

As it is, you are full of your grandiose selves. All such vaunting self-importance is evil. In fact, if you know the right thing to do and don't do it, that, for you, is evil.
—James 4:13–17, MSG

While we are living in this world, each one of us has twenty-four hours each day. That doesn't seem like so much until you break it down and discover it represents 1,440 minutes! That's a lot of minutes ... and we all have the same amount to use. We may have different talents, and the amount of treasure varies from person to person, but we all have the same amount of time. And the basic question I have for you here is: *In what ways are you using the time God has given to you in this world?* Think about that for a few of your valuable minutes. Really! What are you presently using your time for? Are you frantically trying to cram in all of your commitments? Are you spending too much time on frivolous things? Are the things you are pursuing bringing you joy—or exhaustion? And if you are honest, how much of your time are you using up on perishable pursuits, and how much are you investing in God's kingdom for eternal purposes?

Longevity of life is not really the issue here. Some people live very long lives and never accomplish anything of significance while others accomplish a great deal in a very short amount of time. What is important is that we accomplish what we are supposed to in the amount of time we are given.

INTENTIONALITY

In many ways, time is like money. I didn't say time *is* money, I said time is *like* money. It is a resource, a valuable one at that, and it is available to us to use in whatever way we choose.

With money, we all have fixed expenditures: housing, utilities, food, clothing, transportation. Many of us choose a standard of living that uses our money. We don't often think about it in this way, but it's true. After we pay for our fixed expenditures, whatever is left, what I call "discretionary," we use on entertainment, eating out, vacations, and hopefully, ministry. All of this requires *decisions*.

The same is true of our time. We all have fixed "expenditures" with our time: a certain amount of sleep, regular work, eating, including whatever preparation is needed, and obligations to our families. The time we have left we see as discretionary, we can "spend" it on whatever we choose. However, one important factor to consider is that the lifestyle standard that we currently have for our "fixed" expenditures, whether that expenditure is money or time, directly affects what we have "left over."

In what ways are you using the time God has given to you in this world?

If I have a lifestyle that requires a lot of money, there isn't much left over for anything else. If I have a lifestyle that requires a lot of my time, either for work or even a lot of "stuff" to maintain, I won't have a lot of time for other important things. So we see that our discretionary time is also directly affected by the *choices* we make regarding our fixed commitments. We often feel like we don't have any choices, but we always do. Are we thoughtful, disciplined, and intentional with our commitments, or are we just letting them happen?

What possibilities has God put in front of you to use your time for him? Do you see the potential in your circumstances to converterlate your time into eternal treasure? Or is all of your time wrapped up in your own obligations? Do you often postpone making decisions about your time commitments, not because you are being reflective, but because you don't want to really make any changes? Do you put off something really important because something less important takes your focus off of God's call to you? These are important questions! Either we want to converterlate our time ... or we don't.

> **You have potential to converterlate your time into eternal treasure.**

BACK TO BASICS: PERISHABLE VS. IMPERISHABLE

We know that time in this world is a perishable commodity. It is going to run out for each one of us at some point. Our time will have no real meaning in the eternal world, but what we do with it *now* does have an impact on eternity. In the 1960s, Charles Hummel wrote a book entitled, *Tyranny of the Urgent*. The basic premise of this book is that the most *urgent* task is not always the most important. The *tyranny of the urgent* lies in its distortion of priorities. We must evaluate the use of our time not by what is most urgent, but by what is most important. We need discernment to converterlate our perishable time into something imperishable. And we will only have the wisdom that we need for that evaluation if we depend on God and his Word to guide us.

It has become increasingly clear to me that the only two things that will survive the perishable world are the Word of God, which endures forever, and the souls of people, who will live in one of two places for all of eternity. Jesus Christ came into this world to save sinners. When he left this world physically, he left us, his followers, to reach our respective generations with the good news of salvation. One of our responsibilities as believers is to be ambassadors for Christ. The apostle Paul made it clear when he said, "We are therefore Christ's ambassadors, as though God were making his appeal through us" (2 Corinthians 5:20). Each one of us is an ambassador for Christ in one way or another. Our mission is to introduce people to the person of Jesus Christ! How are you using your time to make this happen?

We all know, at least on an intellectual level, that this present world is passing away with all of its attractions. However, why is it that we often don't embrace this reality until we experience a personal crisis? For me, I came face to face with the shortness of my days when I was diagnosed with cancer. It forced me to evaluate the priorities in my life regarding the use of my time. I needed to reconsider my commitments in light of the perishable and imperishable, the temporary and eternal.

In many ways I was using my time to pursue my own kingdom. But as I studied God's Word, I began to see the opportunities before me to make a difference in God's kingdom. I discovered that I needed to use my time to invest in the things God desires.

In the Old Testament we read, "Teach us to number our days that we may get a heart of wisdom" (Psalm 90:12, ESV). As our relationship with God develops and we soak in his Word, he reveals more of himself and his plans for us. As we flow with the Holy Spirit, he empowers us to accomplish God's purposes. God, as the great designer of the entire universe, has a perfect plan for each one of us. *He* is the one who knows how we should use our time and what will bring us joy. Transformed *KingdomNomics* thinkers remind themselves that we have a limited amount of time to make an impact on this world and the world to come. Our natural desire to simply spend our time on the values of this world must be transformed into a desire to make a difference in eternity.

BEWARE: THE CHIEF CONSUMERLATOR WANTS YOUR TIME

At the very most, Satan wants to use our time for his benefit, and at the very least, he wants to keep us from using our time in the way in which God wants us to. The Chief Consumerlator will use whatever means he has available to keep us from doing God's will. We must remember that time is a currency that needs to be invested in the right things.

I have found that many people attempt to find fulfillment in life in the wrong ways and in the wrong places as they follow wrong pursuits. They think that the pleasure of this world, whether it is found in relationships, work, recreation, or pastimes, will provide the meaning in life that they so desperately wish to experience. Often, time used in this way simply results in disappointment, disillusionment, regret, depression, or even despair.

> **Time is a currency that needs to be invested in the right things.**

One of the priorities we often fail to make time for is our relationships. Time invested in people will always reap dividends. However, many people make the mistake of investing their time in things that offer an immediate sense of satisfaction, but that in the long term damage their relationships with those who should be the closest to them. An example of someone who fails to properly converterlate their time into establishing relationships is the business person who consumes too much of their time on a career at the expense of their marriage and family. No one lying on their deathbed ever said they should have spent more time on their business career in exchange for their family relationships. The regret is the other way around. They wish they had spent more time with their loved ones. We need God's wisdom to avoid falling prey to Satan's subtle deceit.

The book of Isaiah tells us, "If you spend yourselves in behalf of the hungry and satisfy the needs of the oppressed, then your light will rise in the darkness, and your night will become like the noonday. The Lord will guide you always; he will satisfy your needs in a sun-scorched land and will strengthen your frame. You will be like a well-watered garden, like a spring whose waters never fail" (Isaiah 58:10–11). When I think of a "well-watered garden" or a "spring whose waters never fail," I think of something with vitality and creativity and beauty. If I apply this metaphor to a person, I think of someone who is energetic, and focused, and alive. Are you that person? Or are you a sun-scorched garden or a spring that has gone dry. I encounter a lot of people who are tired. They are busy. They are weary. And they are frustrated that their lives are not producing anything of substance, let alone something that will last for all eternity. Satan has confused their priorities. The Chief Consumerlator will make you *too* busy and will find a way to rob you of your joy and life if you are not careful.

The Chief Consumerlator will also use guilt to immobilize us. I'm not referring to the good kind of guilt that brings us to repentance for our sins. I'm talking about the false guilt that is simply fear of disapproval. Sometimes people experience false guilt when they use their resources for anything other than God's eternal purposes. The question people often ask me is: How much time can I use for "myself"? They are referring to the discretionary time that we discussed earlier. There are many good things that we have to enjoy: TV, sports, entertainment, social media. The important thing to remember here is that there is not a formula for using our time. It is critical that we evaluate on a regular basis how we are using our time, but we also must know that God leads each one of us differently in each chapter (or season) of our lives according to how he designed us individually. How do we balance our time between our various responsibilities? We seek God's wisdom! In Ephesians 5 we read, "Carefully determine what pleases the Lord ... Be careful how you live ... Make the most of every opportunity" (Ephesians 5:10–16, NLT). We need to rely on our relationship with God and his guidance.

FINDING BALANCE

There is a difference between using time for refreshment and renewal, which all of us need from time to time, and wasting time on pleasure. There are many ways to relax and enjoy life, however there needs to be balance in this area. We need refreshment; however, we need to carefully exercise discernment in order to make sure we are not just being a consumerlator instead of a Converterlator.

I say this because when I was younger, for me the epitome of "living" was to be on the golf course. I would grab every moment I could to be there. I loved everything about that lifestyle. However, my desire for that way of life from a time standpoint began to fade as I exposed myself more and more to the truth of God's Word. As my desire to spend more time in the Word grew, I began to see my excessive time on the golf course as purely selfish. As I spent more time studying the Bible and learning how to soak, sow, and flow with the Spirit, I was impressed with the need to converterlate my time for the achievement of eternal purposes. This included preparation time for teaching Sunday school classes, which actually also benefitted me so much personally. I began to think about how I could use the secular talents that God has given to me for eternal purposes.

When we start thinking this way, our goals and motivations begin to change as God calls us to move in different directions in our new life with him. I began to aspire to be on the King's team, and to really be an impact player for helping to fulfill the Great Commission. My time on the golf course began to have less allure. Our world has a lot of perishable distractions to offer us! Sometimes those perishable distractions are actually "good" things: sports, work, relationships, hobbies. We need these things, but we also need to be careful in how we use our time. The question always remains: *Where is your focus?*

The world says "indulge"; God says "do my will." We must set our sights beyond the deceptions of our culture. We need to experience relaxation and pleasure in the way God intends. In the book of Ecclesiastes, we discover that King Solomon used his time to pursue many good things, but because his focus was outside of God's purpose, all of those pursuits became meaningless to him. We must always keep in mind that we will only find joy and purpose in our relationships and accomplishments within the context of God's purpose for our lives. And it is only within the context of a future eternity that all of these things make sense.

Are you carefully and intentionally using the specific time that God has given you?

We find true fulfillment when we discover what we have been designed for and then use our time in conformance to that design. This does not mean that we need to be busier. It means that we need to carefully and intentionally use the specific time that God has given us. What opportunities has God recently given you to use your time for him? Ask the Holy Spirit to open your heart and mind to God's direction in this area of your life, and then act on what he shows you!

Converterlating Your Time:

Use some of your time to think about these questions and redirect the converterlating of your time:

- How am I currently using the time God has given to me, really?
- How much of my time am I using on perishable pursuits?
- How much of my time am I investing in God's kingdom?
- How much of my time is "fixed"? How much "discretionary" time do I have?
- Am I typically thoughtful about my time commitments or do I just let them "happen"? How can I be more intentional about investing my time?
- How do I typically respond to the opportunities that God puts in front of me to use my time for his kingdom?
- If I am honest, do I really *want* to converterlate my time for God's kingdom? If the answer is yes, what am I willing to do to make that happen?

12

CONVERTERLATING YOUR TALENT

I beseech you therefore, brethren, by the mercies of God, that you present your bodies a living sacrifice, holy, acceptable to God, which is your reasonable service.
—Romans 12:1, NKJV

A paper weight on my desk has the inscription, "Don't wait for your ship to come in. Swim out to it!" As we practice *KingdomNomics*, we aggressively look for ways to converterlate our talents for the advancement of the kingdom of God. People often make the mistake of waiting for their ship to come in, hoping for something to come their way. Waiting and wishing with good intentions will not accomplish any worthwhile objective. If it feels like not much is happening in your life, perhaps the Lord is saying, "Stop waiting for your ship; start swimming!"

We need to be alert to areas in which the Holy Spirit is moving us and blessing the efforts we are making on his behalf. Then we have to "swim" out to those places and join the forward movement with the rest of the team.

> **Waiting and wishing with good intentions will not accomplish any worthwhile objective.**

Someone once said it is a lot easier to steer a moving car than one that is standing still. As we participate in worthwhile kingdom efforts, we can more easily see how the Lord is guiding us to the places where we can be the most productive.

A LITTLE CAN BE A LOT

Right about now, you may be thinking: How do I know how, when, where, and what to do in order to do my part in what is such a huge undertaking? This, in some ways, was the attitude of the disciples when it came to the feeding of the 5,000, "Here is a boy with five small barley loaves and two small fish, but how far will they go among so many?" (John 6:9). We do not know much about the little boy; but we do see that he was the right boy in the right place on that day, and he was willing to offer whatever he had to Jesus. The disciples, on the other hand, were bewildered and didn't know where or how to start.

In some ways the loaves and fish were the boy's "treasure." But I think as we consider the use of our talents, the loaves and fish also represent all that we have to give in service to our King. Fortunately for the young lad, he was willing to release what he had in his hands to the Lord for the use of kingdom purposes at that time. God is in the business of taking what is seemingly small and insignificant, and exponentially multiplying whatever it is to accomplish his purposes. We do not hear of this boy again in Scripture, but his gift to God and the blessing of it has been read by millions of people. He used what he had where he was and God used it in a powerful way. Ephesians 3:20 tells us, "Now to him who is able to do immeasurably more than all we ask or imagine, according to his power that is at work within us." God's power is at work within *each one of us*. It doesn't matter what talent we do or do not have, God's power will work in us to accomplish more than we can imagine.

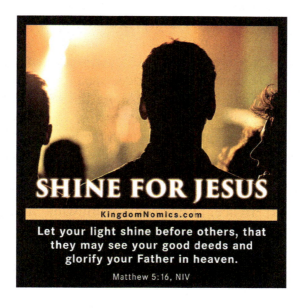

As I was studying this passage of Scripture, I considered my own life. What had God given to me? Well, he had blessed me financially. And that financial blessing was the result of fortunate business and investment transactions over the years. I realized that my business sense could be used for the advancement of God's kingdom if I would be willing to converterlate those abilities for the use of kingdom endeavors. So I decided to convert both my time and my talent into an investment in the imperishable values of the kingdom. My desire to do that now trumps the desire to use my material resources on the perishable items of this world. Sometimes I call myself a "financial farmer" who grows money with a mission. I love doing it, and it is thrilling to use my talent in this way. I always remember, God is the one who has shown me and taught me, and he is the source of any increase that comes my way. I always acknowledge that, and I humbly express my gratitude to him for it.

God has opened doors of opportunity to share what I have learned and experienced on a scale I never thought would be possible. Along the way, he has brought a number of individuals across my path who have unique talents and skills in the use of today's communication technologies not even in existence a few years ago. These people have enabled me, a person with no name, and no platform, and with very little experience, to develop a worldwide ministry designed to share these wonderful secrets of the kingdom with tens of thousands of people. I have also encountered people who have no platform from a secular standpoint, and who have access to only limited resources, and yet they are using their talents with technology to reach millions of people with the message of Christ. Whatever we have, God can take it and exponentially multiply it for the expansion of his kingdom and glory.

It is important for us to understand that each one of us has a sphere of influence. We all have people we interact with on a regular basis. God has not just given us abilities; he has also placed each one of us into a specific setting with the opportunity to influence people for his eternal purposes. We all have places that we go where God can use us. We need to depend on the Holy Spirit to show us how and where our talents and abilities can not only be a blessing to others, but can make a difference for eternity.

> **Whatever we have, God can take it and exponentially multiply it.**

Do not belittle whatever God has given to you. He is in the business of generating much out of little or nothing. Remember, the lad brought little to the "field of play," but he left with a lot more than he brought to the game.

YOUR SPECIAL DESIGN

God has created each one of us for a unique mission and he has equipped us with the exact abilities and talents to accomplish that mission. In the Old Testament we read, "I knew you before I formed you in your mother's womb. Before you were born I set you apart" (Jeremiah 1:5, NLT). The most powerful, wise, and loving being in the entire universe personally shaped us. God set us apart for a special purpose while we were still in our mother's womb.

Recently I was presented with some information that relates directly to this topic. We can use the acronym SPECIAL to consider the talents and abilities God has given each one of us. Your SPECIAL design includes:

Spiritual Gifts

> As each one has received a special gift, employ it in serving one another, as good stewards of the manifold grace of God.
> —1 Peter 4:10, NASB

At the time that we accept Jesus Christ as our Lord and Savior, the Holy Spirit gives each of us one or more spiritual gifts. It is the Holy Spirit who determines which gift or gifts we receive. These spiritual gifts are different from the natural abilities a person already possesses at the time of their spiritual birth. These gifts equip us for special service within the body of Christ. The Holy Spirit has spiritually gifted *you* for a unique role and mission.

> **The Holy Spirit has spiritually gifted *you* for a unique role and mission.**

Often times our strengths and special gifts are identified and confirmed by others. We can't always see them because they are a normal part of our lives, but the fact is, *each one of us* is gifted.

What spiritual gifts can you identify in your life? Are you using these gifts to serve others in the body of Christ and to make a deposit in the Bank of Heaven?

Personality Traits

> When the time came for her to give birth, there were twin boys in her womb ... The boys grew up, and Esau became a skillful hunter, a man of the open country, while Jacob was content to stay at home.
> —Genesis 25:24, 27

We are born with different personalities. These personal qualities affect how we think, what we value, and what we do. For example, some people are naturally aggressive while others are passive. Some like adventure and variety while others prefer stability and routine. Some are reserved while others are outgoing. There are many more traits that are blended into various personality combinations. While you were still in your mother's womb, God designed a personality for you that is perfectly suited for his plan for your life. While the world may value certain personality types more than others, God has designed each and every person with their own personality, and he can use those personalities in a powerful way.

What are the personal qualities that God has included in your temperament? In what ways do you see the Holy Spirit using the strengths *and* weaknesses of your personality?

Extraordinary Background

> A person's steps are directed by the Lord. How then can anyone understand their own way?
> —Proverbs 20:24

The experiences of our lives have a profound impact on the kind of people we become. Our family roots, our educational opportunities, our vocational history, the friendships and acquaintances we've made, and the major life events that we've experienced all combine to give us a totally unique background. God orchestrates the events and circumstances of our lives so we will have the knowledge, relationships, and experiences necessary to fulfill our individual missions in life.

What are the major events, experiences, and relationships in your past that have influenced the way you are today? How is God using your past circumstances, positive and negative, to transform your life and accomplish his purposes?

Central Motivation

> I focus on this one thing: Forgetting the past and looking forward to what lies ahead, I press on to reach the end of the race and receive the heavenly prize for which God, through Christ Jesus, is calling us.
> —Philippians 3:13–14, NLT

There are many different motivations that drive us. However, in each person there are one or two primary drives that exceed all the others. These central motivations provide the emotional heartbeat for each person. We've all encountered people who appear to be tireless when they are involved in activities that satisfy this motivational thrust. A central motivation is a God-given drive that he built into you. It's what makes you, you! Think about that for a moment. What excites you, or inspires you, or stimulates you to get involved in something? Your central motivation includes your abilities, your interests, the circumstances in which you are most productive, the relationships that bring out the best in you, and what kind of end result brings you the most joy. All of these factors fit together to give us a motivational pattern. As we discern what our motivation is, each one of us needs to focus that drive toward God's eternal purposes. Without the proper focus your central motivation can quickly propel you toward perishable pursuits that are not part of God's plan for you.

What is *your* central motivation? Are you using your drive to pursue perishable or imperishable things?

Inherited Abilities

> All who are skilled among you are to come and make everything the Lord has commanded."
> —Exodus 35:10

Different people have different inherited abilities. These natural abilities enable us to do certain things well. For example, some people are athletic, some are musical, some are artistic, and some are mechanical. Some people have an aptitude for working with numbers, while others are better with words. Some have natural people skills while others have a knack for training animals. The abilities that you have were not randomly assigned. God has given you inherited abilities so you can better serve him and his kingdom.

What are your natural abilities? How is God using your abilities to accomplish his purposes?

Approved Adversity

> Consider it pure joy, my brothers and sisters, whenever you face trials of many kinds, because you know that the testing of your faith produces perseverance. Let perseverance finish its work so that you may be mature and complete, not lacking anything."
> —James 1:2–4

Do you find it hard to believe that God was instrumental in putting you in your circumstances? What about the things that you have always disliked about how you are made? Did God also permit those apparent imperfections for a reason?

> As Jesus was walking along, he saw a man who had been blind from birth. "Rabbi," his disciples asked him, "why was this man born

> blind? Was it because of his own sins or his parents' sins?"

> "It was not because of his sins or his parents' sins," Jesus answered. "This happened so the power of God could be seen in him."
> —John 9:1–3, NLT

We are not mutant creations. God has intentionally made each one of us for a special purpose! However, that doesn't mean that all things will be easy. Adversity is one of the tools used by God to shape us into usable vessels. Adversity plays a major role in the kind of person we become. While we bring some adversity upon ourselves through disobedience, God uses even that to mold us.

> And we know that for those who love God all things work together for good, for those who are called according to his purpose.
> —Romans 8:28, ESV

Sometimes God allows trials into our lives to build our character and enable us to minister to others who face similar difficulties. God's approved adversity increases in direct proportion to the size and significance of the mission for which he is preparing you.

What are the painful, difficult situations or hardships that have impacted you up to this point in your life? How is God using this adversity to develop you as a person and to minister to others?

Lifelong Mission

> For we are his workmanship, created in Christ Jesus for good works, which God prepared beforehand, that we should walk in them.
> —Ephesians 2:10, ESV

God has given you a special design because he has assigned you a special mission. The good works that God planned for you to do also make you different from everybody else. There are certain things that God has chosen you to do and he has custom designed you so you can do them better than anyone else. God wants you to participate in the plan that he has crafted for your life, but it's up to you as to whether or not you will do them.

Have you identified your special mission? What special things do you see God accomplishing through you?

These are the various facets of your SPECIAL design. You are totally unique. There is no one like you. And that didn't happen by chance; it happened by the ingenious design of our Creator.

ARE YOU AVAILABLE?

Each one of us needs to ask ourselves this question: *Am I available?*

If we are really honest, oftentimes, we are *un*available.

This was also true in Bible times. Moses didn't want to go to Egypt to be the spokesman for leading the people out of the Egyptian captivity. He offered all kinds of excuses. Gideon questioned why God would choose him to head up the army that would free God's people from their oppressors. Jonah ran away from the responsibility God called him to. John Mark deserted Paul and Barnabas on a missionary journey.

God is looking for *available* people to do his work. Jesus said, "The harvest is great, but the workers are few" (Matthew 9:37, NLT). When it comes to investing your talent, are you willing to allow God to use all of your abilities and gifts for his purposes, no matter what that may be?

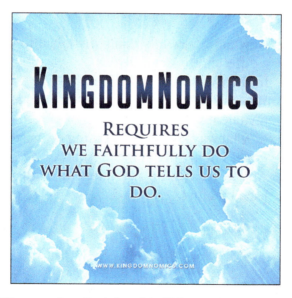

The prophet Isaiah said, "Then I heard the Lord asking, 'Whom should I send as a messenger to this people? Who will go for us?' I said, 'Here I am. Send me'" (Isaiah 6:8, NLT). What opportunities is God giving you to use your talent to serve him? The Holy Spirit has empowered us to accomplish great things. Second Corinthians 5:5 encourages us with these words, "He who has prepared us for this very thing is God, who has given us the Spirit" (ESV). You may have many talents or only one, but with the Holy Spirit's power working through you, you can make a difference that will last for all eternity.

Converterlating Your Talent:

Consider these questions and maximize the converterlating of your talent:

- How am I currently using my talent to make a difference for eternity?
- In what ways am I SPECIAL?
- What steps do I need to take to converterlate my talent for God's kingdom?
- In what ways is (can) God using my past experiences in my life at the present?
- Am I offering up my talent to God to be used by him?

13

CONVERTERLATING YOUR TREASURE

"Whoever sows sparingly will also reap sparingly, and whoever sows generously will also reap generously. Each of you should give what you have decided in your heart to give, not reluctantly or under compulsion, for God loves a cheerful giver. And God is able to bless you abundantly, so that in all things at all times, having all that you need, you will abound in every good work."
—2 Corinthians 9:6-8

A few years ago, my wife and I drove through the entrance of our condominium complex at night, and I complained to her about how the street lamps were shining in different colors unevenly. I said, "The lighting here makes the neighborhood look terrible. At the next board meeting of the condo association, I am going to complain about it and tell them to fix up the lighting."

A few weeks later, I did exactly that. I stood up in the board meeting in a room full of people to inform them the lighting should be changed. I told them they needed to get evenly lighted bulbs of the same color for all of the lampposts. I remember thinking it was odd that I was receiving a number of perplexed looks from both the board members and the members of the condo association who were in attendance.

Not long after giving my dissertation at that meeting on how the condominium lighting needed to be changed, I had cataract surgery and the doctor implanted new lenses in my eyes. Well, you can guess what happened! The new lenses gave me 20/20 vision on both intermediate and long-distance vision along with a sharpness that I had never before experienced in my life!

A few days later we drove into the condominium complex in the evening and I said to my wife, "Wow! The condominium board sure moved quickly. They changed the lighting. It is really bright, almost too bright. But they didn't change to the amber color I suggested."

Bless her heart, Ruth Ann started to laugh. She said, "They haven't changed any of the lighting. It is the same as it was before!" I started to laugh, too.

> **In what ways has your relationship with Jesus Christ transformed the way you use your earthly treasure?**

My vision was changed! No wonder everyone at the meeting had looked at me in a funny way. Then I wondered whether I should go back to the board and apologize for my mistaken view of things!

I share this experience to illustrate how a relationship with Christ changes our perspective on all things, including how we use our treasure. We have a distorted view of the world because of sin. Jesus comes into our lives and we see things in a different way. Before Christ came into my life, I had one view of money—it was meant to be used for my own personal pleasure. My perception was as if I were seeing my earthly treasure through a pair of eyes before my cataract operation. My view was distorted. Everything I thought was important was diametrically opposed to the things of God. I needed the perspective of eternity. In what ways has your relationship with Jesus Christ transformed the way you use your earthly treasure?

CHANGED PERSPECTIVE LEADS TO CONVERTERLATING

In my first book, I shared how I went through a conversion process. My relationship with Jesus Christ set me on the road to becoming a Converterlator. This is a journey for each one of us and God teaches us and leads us in many different ways. However, the one thing I do know is that each one of us is called to converterlate our time, talent, and treasure. Now that my life is directed by God, I have a different view of all of my earthly treasure including my money and I use it in a different way than I did before I met Christ. My goal is to be investing in eternity.

I love the story of Zacchaeus in the New Testament. In Luke 19 we read, "And when Jesus came to the place, he looked up and said to him, 'Zacchaeus, hurry and come down, for I must stay at your house today.' So [Zacchaeus] hurried and came down and received him joyfully" (Luke 19:5–6, ESV).

> **Each one of us is called to converterlate our time, talent, and treasure.**

Zacchaeus was a "money guy" who was hated by his own people because he was a tax collector for the notorious Roman government. He was a self-starter, and he really did not care what other people thought of him. But here we find him wanting to see Jesus! He found a tree that would put him above the crowd and he waited. When Jesus called him, he responded immediately.

In verse 8 we read the rest of the story: "And Zacchaeus stood and said to the Lord, 'Behold, Lord, the half of my goods I give to the poor. And if I have defrauded anyone of anything, I restore it fourfold'" (ESV). The life of Zacchaeus was *changed*! His encounter with Jesus transformed the view he had of his wealth *and* of his fellow man. The Spirit enlightened his heart and moved him to follow through with his new insight. By giving away a large portion of his personal wealth he became a strategic kingdom investor. He finally understood that his money was to be used for the advancement of God's kingdom, not his own, and he responded! When his perspective changed, so did his behavior. Are you using *your* material blessings to bless other people?

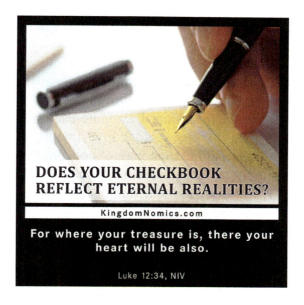

A STRATEGIC KINGDOM INVESTOR

Over the years I have learned to be a *strategic* kingdom investor. This means that I am increasingly careful where I invest funds for the expansion of the kingdom. I *strategically* plan and choose where my kingdom treasure is to be invested.

On a practical level, in the investment world, it has been my observation that many intelligent investors make it a practice to invest in things that have "intrinsic" value. This means converting dollars, and other paper currencies, into material things like gold, silver, and to a lesser extent into companies that pay dividends. They like to invest in companies that have "hard assets" or facilities that are hard to duplicate. These things do not lose their value over the years. Wise investors work to find assets that will be an adequate store of lasting value.

I believe "hard assets" for a Christ-follower are found in what will last for eternity. Personally, I like to invest in ministries focusing on the fulfillment of the Great Commission. I evaluate each ministry like I do many of my secular investments. I look for high-impact ministries with exponential factors causing them to multiply. Ministries that meet the physical, material, and spiritual needs of people in the name of Christ are of great interest to me and my family. Normally, we only invest with those with whom we have had long-term relationships because we know how they use and administer their funding for the greatest possible kingdom returns.

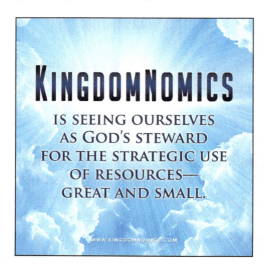

Here are a few general questions to ask as you consider investing your money or other material resources in a ministry or organization:

1. Does this organization exalt Jesus Christ above all else?
2. Does this ministry have a record of spiritual fruitfulness?
3. Does this organization seek to use perishable means to accomplish imperishable results?
4. Does this ministry exhibit documented financial accountability and transparency?
5. Do you trust the people involved in this ministry to conscientiously use the resources you are entrusting to them?

As you consider the above questions, ask the Holy Spirit to give you discernment so that you are able to make wise decisions when you are investing your earthly treasure.

I have found that when we strategically invest time, talent, and treasure in other people, sometimes mutually beneficial relationships can be established that will last a long time. Here's one example from my own life. I remember God leading me to make a small investment in a company that was of particular interest to a very successful businessman in the early days of my business career. Little did I realize at the time what that would mean for me personally.

Shortly after making that investment, I started receiving phone calls from this man, and we established a friendly business relationship. Soon, he made it clear to me he was going to open several doors of opportunity to me. For some reason, he took an interest in me, and he became my business mentor. In time he mentioned to others in my presence that I was a protégé of his. He advised me throughout most of my business career. This happened simply because I showed an interest in what he was interested in by converting some of my time and money into an interest of his. God often blesses us in surprising ways when we strategically use our treasure to honor him.

WEAVING A PATTERN OF GIVING INTO YOUR LIVING

Each person has a different financial situation. In many parts of the world people have very little in the way of financial resources. It is important for all of us to remember that God loves the *cheerful* giver. In 2 Corinthians 9:7 we read, "Each one must give as he has decided in his heart, not reluctantly or under compulsion, for God loves a cheerful giver" (ESV). God is more interested in the attitude we have about our giving than in the amount we give. All that we have has been given to us by God. Are we joyfully allowing him to use it to bless those around us? Are people welcome in your home? Do you share what you do have without being self-conscious that others may have more or less than you do? Are you willing to share what you have without being concerned about receiving a "thank you" in return? Do you consider the eternal ramifications of your giving?

My goal is to be a grace giver, empowered by the Holy Spirit. Grace-giving is the result of a God-given and God-driven desire to give following three basic principles: he who sows bountifully will reap bountifully, what is reasonable to give to a particular project considering your current life circumstances, and how much can be given to this project cheerfully? The Bible tells us that when we sow bountifully, we will reap bountifully (2 Corinthians 9:6). God gives us the *choice* of sowing sparingly or bountifully. In Luke 21:1–4 (and in Mark 12:41–44) we read about the poor widow who "out of her poverty put in all she had to live on" as a freewill offering into the temple treasury, which amounted to two small copper coins. This was all that she had and yet she sowed it bountifully. Hers was a gift of sacrifice; nevertheless, she gave it generously and sacrificially. This was low-profile giving at its best! The value of what we give to God's work is not determined by its amount, but by the spirit in which we give it. God will surely bless whatever we give to him with a heart of gratitude, generosity, and expectancy that he will use it to further his kingdom. When it comes to giving I often use the acronym GIVE to remind me of the important principles that need to guide my giving:

G Grace-giving is the result of my God-given, God-driven desire to give.
I I desire to give because my giving is a major gateway for God to work in my life.
V Victory over self; my desire to invest in the imperishable trumps my desire to invest in the perishable.
E Eyes are fixed on the unseen and eternal rewards.

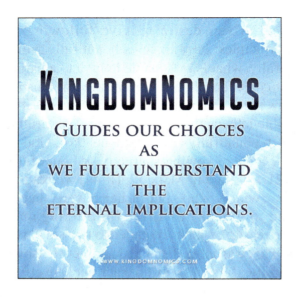

Before my one-hundred-year-old aunt died, she shared with me a saying she had learned in the first grade: "A habit is like a cable. We weave it one strand each day until it becomes so strong, it cannot be broken."

I told her I really liked that saying, and that I would change the word "habit" to the word "faith" making the saying, "Faith is like a cable. We weave it one strand each day until it becomes so strong, it cannot be broken."

However, I think this saying can also have the word "habit" replaced by the word "giving," making it, "Giving is like a cable. We weave it one strand each day until it becomes so strong, it cannot be broken." We need to weave our giving into the fabric of our lives to the point that our practice of giving cannot be broken. Truly, this is one of the secrets of the kingdom

I continue to learn about. Giving is the major gateway by which God gets involved in the life of the believer. We will increasingly see "the finger of God" at work in our circumstances and otherwise when we practice giving our treasure to the interests of the kingdom.

Converterlating Your Treasure:

Take time to answer these questions to consider how you can better converterlate your treasure:

- In what ways am I currently using whatever earthly treasure I have to accomplish things of eternal consequence?
- How can I use my earthly treasure to bless others and achieve eternal treasure?
- Have I ever considered a *strategic* approach to my giving? How might more thoughtful, intentional giving reap greater eternal benefits and rewards?
- What opportunities has God placed before me as I invest the treasure he has blessed me with?

14

Your Echo into Eternity

Therefore do not throw away your confidence, which has a great reward. For you have need of endurance, so that when you have done the will of God you may receive what is promised.
—Hebrews 10:35–36, ESV

A reward time *is* coming. There *is* a time when each one of us will stand in front of the Judgment Seat of Christ for the purpose of receiving reward or suffering loss of reward. We *do* have accountability to the Lord for what we have done or not done here on this earth. Jesus Christ is coming back, and he is bringing a reward with him. The apostle Paul had a lot to say on this topic in the New Testament. Here are just two examples from his letters to the Corinthians:

For this light momentary affliction is preparing for us an eternal weight of glory beyond all comparison.
—2 Corinthians 4:17, ESV

For no one can lay a foundation other than that which is laid, which is Jesus Christ. Now if anyone builds on the foundation with gold, silver, precious stones, wood, hay, straw— each one's work will become manifest, for the Day will disclose it, because it will be revealed by fire, and the fire will test what sort of work each one has done. If the work that anyone has built on the foundation survives, he will receive a reward. If anyone's work is burned up, he will suffer loss, though he himself will be saved, but only as through fire.
—1 Corinthians 3:11–15, ESV

Only to the extent that we build our lives on the foundation of Christ, by allowing him to live his life through us, can we expect the deeds we do in the body to be able to stand the test of fire. Is your treasure on earth or in heaven? Are you living your life in such a way as to maximize your opportunities so that your life will echo into eternity?

God's grace in many ways prioritizes opportunity. We serve the God who provides the opportunity to each one of us to respond to his grace. He is the God who draws us to himself through his Son Jesus Christ. He creates in us an increasing desire to invest in the imperishable values of his eternal kingdom. For those who respond to the opportunities he presents to us, the future is one of glory beyond human description to be enjoyed in his presence forever.

There is a message to those of us who are on the King's team, "Wake up, sleeper, rise from the dead, and Christ will shine on you" (Ephesians 5:14). The time is short, and the eternal destinies of multitudes are at stake. We need to wake up and get busy doing the King's business. If we follow this exhortation, Christ will shine on our lives. And when Christ shines on our lives, things happen!

We all have opportunities to build our eternal treasure, and the message to us is clear: We need

> **When Christ shines on our lives, things happen!**

to respond properly to the message of God, we need to reach for the best that God has to offer, and we need to press on toward the heavenly goal God has for us. Prayer, the Word of God, and the power of the Holy Spirit will deliver us from the wiles of the consumerlator so that we can develop into the Converterlators God has planned for us to be.

God is giving each one of us an opportunity to be an eternal "star." In both the Old and New Testaments we read, "Those who are wise will shine like the brightness of the heavens, and those who lead many to righteousness, like the stars for ever and ever" (Daniel 12:3); and "Then the righteous will shine like the sun in the kingdom of their Father" (Matthew 13:43).

Most of us are not "great" people in the eyes of the world. From a kingdom perspective, this gives us an advantage. God often uses the weak among us to accomplish great things. Each day is a new opportunity for us to serve him. Each new day is an opportunity to strategically invest our time, talent, and treasure into things of eternal value.

You and I have been given the opportunity to be a member of the King's Team. It is a great time to be alive in the history of the world! The Bible tells us, "Therefore, since we are surrounded by such a great cloud of witnesses, let us throw off everything that hinders and the sin that so easily entangles. And let us run with perseverance the race marked out for us, fixing our eyes on Jesus, the pioneer and perfecter of faith. For the joy set before him he endured the cross, scorning its shame, and sat down at the right hand of the throne of God" (Hebrews 12:1–2).

The question is, *Are we spiritually astute enough to see this time as a time of eternal opportunity?* The stakes are high. The eternal destinies of multitudes are at stake. Every player is needed. We are in the army of God! We do not want to miss the opportunities to be low-profile, high-impact players on the King's Team. We are playing for imperishable crowns to bring glory to the King of Kings.

In Matthew 6:20, Jesus tells us to "lay up for yourselves treasures in heaven" (ESV). Yes, we can have an eternal 401k. Yes, our treasure can last forever. It is guaranteed. The returns are fantastic; in fact, they are beyond our human ability to measure.

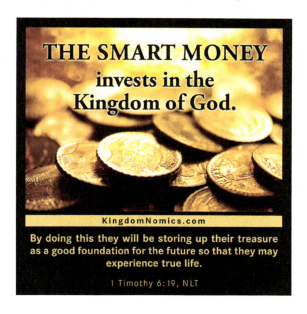

In this world many people follow "stock tips." They pursue what they perceive to be "smart money" and invest in companies for which they have little or no information. Most of the time, this type of investing results in losses. Jesus, however, gives us a sure "eternal investment tip." He says we should invest our resources in treasure in heaven. We can take it with us if we send it ahead by investing in the imperishable world to come while we are still in this perishing world. The "smart money" is going into the kingdom of God.

Yes, there are obstacles and it gets tough out there, but by the Holy Spirit's power we can stay focused on the eternal rewards of being in the game. My prayer is that each one of us will capture the vision and run with the mission in order to help fulfill the Great Commission. Let's encourage each other to use our time, talent, and treasure effectively in this world; eternity is on the horizon. It is approaching us at warp speed!

Look, I am coming soon! My reward is with me, and I will give to each person according to what they have done.
I am the Alpha and the Omega, the First and the Last, the Beginning and the End.
(Revelation 22:12–13)

To him who is able to keep you from stumbling and to present you before his glorious presence without fault and with great joy

*to the only God our Savior be glory, majesty, power
and authority,
through Jesus Christ our Lord, before all ages,
now and forevermore! Amen.*
(Jude 24–25)

Appendix A

KingdomNomics DNA

The DNA markers of those who practice the concepts of *KingdomNomics* differ radically from those who abide by the "wisdom" promoted by the world system. *KingdomNomics* thinkers:

… focus their lives on the person of Jesus Christ.
… understand that they have been given a "loaf of time" that is being shortened by a slice each day.
… recognize that they live in a time bubble that can pop at any time.
… embrace their SPECIAL design by God and live for all his purposes.
… apply the core concepts of *soak, sow, and flow* to their lives on a daily basis.
… realize their "three Ts"—time, talent, and treasure—are resources at risk of being consumed by perishable goals in this temporary world.
… discover that they can convert their perishable resources into imperishable treasure that will echo into eternity.

... see Christ living in and through them by the work of the Holy Spirit.
... believe that God works through the grace-giving principles outlined in 2 Corinthians 9, "And God is able to bless you abundantly, so that in all things at all times, having all that you need, you will abound in every good work" (2 Corinthians 9:8).
... practice giving while they are living.
... are strategic kingdom investors striving to meet the spiritual, physical, and material needs of people in the name of Jesus Christ for the purpose of helping to fulfill the Great Commission.

When these principles are active in our lives, we will experience God's power working in and through us in a mighty way. We will be active Converterlators, using all of our time, talent, and treasure for the advancement of God's kingdom.

Appendix B

KingdomNomics Gospel Presentation

The key to living your life by *KingdomNomics* principles is to make sure you have a living and personal relationship with Jesus Christ. Once this relationship is established, the living and powerful Word of God can begin to work in your life as you practice the principles of *KingdomNomics*.

Let's take a walk together through a few verses of the Bible to show us how we can be sure we have the living relationship God wants us to have with Jesus Christ. It is through Jesus Christ that life and immortality have been brought to light giving us the option to enjoy a life now that will echo into eternity.

On the following pages you will find a scriptural explanation of how you can enter into a personal relationship with Jesus Christ that will truly make a difference for all of eternity. This is the most important decision you will ever make.

What Jesus Christ Did For Us

The apostle Paul said,

> I passed on to you what was most important and what had also been passed on to me. Christ died for our sins, just as the Scriptures said. He was buried, and he was raised from the dead on the third day, just as the Scriptures said. He was seen by Peter and then by the Twelve. After that, he was seen by more than 500 of his followers at one time, most of whom are still alive, though some have died.
> —1 Corinthians 15:3–6, NLT

This is the gospel. It is of first importance that we understand, accept, believe, and trust in the fact that Jesus Christ died for our sins and God raised him from the dead on the third day. The apostle Paul tells us this is the reason Jesus came into the world,

> What I say is true, and you should fully accept it: Christ Jesus came into the world to save sinners, of whom I am the worst.
> —1 Timothy 1:15, NCV

Jesus Christ Provides the Only Way to the Father

> Jesus answered, "I am the way, and the truth, and the life. The only way to the Father is through me."
> —John 14:6, NCV

> I am the gate; whoever enters through me will be saved. They will come in and go out, and find pasture.
> —John 10:9

I Am Accepted and Obtain Right Standing with God:

… When I agree with God that I am a sinner.

I have failed to be what God wants me to be, and I have failed to do what God wants me to do. Therefore, I qualify as a sinner in the sight of God; I have failed to meet his standard of righteousness.

> For everyone has sinned; we all fall short of God's glorious standard.
> —Romans 3:23, NLT

… When I understand that sin, if not paid for, will result in death.

The Bible makes it clear that because God is holy, he cannot overlook my sin. However, he has made provision for the payment of my sin through his Son, Jesus Christ.

> The payment for sin is death. But God gives us the free gift of life forever in Christ Jesus our Lord.
> —Romans 6:23, NCV

My salvation is in the person of Jesus Christ, and it is a *free gift* to me if I will personally receive it by faith.

> Yet we know that a person is made right with God not by following the law, but by trusting in Jesus Christ. So we, too, have put our faith in Christ Jesus, that we might be made right with God because we trusted in Christ. It is not because we followed the law, because no one can be made right with God by following the law.
> —Galatians 2:16, NCV

… When I am made right with God by trusting in Jesus Christ alone for my salvation.

Eternal life is in Jesus Christ, and it is a free gift given to me by God. I must not trust in myself, my good works, behavior, giving or any other works for my salvation.

> This is what God told us: God has given us eternal life, and this life is in his Son. Whoever has the Son has life, but whoever does not have the Son of God does not have life.
> —1 John 5:11–12, NCV

Now …

If you openly declare that Jesus is Lord and believe in your heart that God raised him

from the dead, you will be saved. For it is by believing in your heart that you are made right with God, and it is by openly declaring your faith that you are saved.
—Romans 10:9–10, NLT

Pray this prayer:

Lord Jesus, I confess you are Lord. I believe in my heart you died for my sins, and that God raised you from the dead. I am trusting in you alone for my salvation, not my works, behavior, or anything else. By faith, I ask you to be my Lord and Savior. I thank you for your gift of eternal life. I invite you, Lord Jesus, into my heart to take control of how I think, feel, and act. Thank you for doing so. In your name, I pray. Amen.

God's Guarantee

If you sincerely prayed this prayer believing that Jesus Christ is your personal Lord and Savior, you are now secure in him with the guarantee of going to heaven. The following verses, along with many others found in the Bible, give us the assurance that our salvation is a present possession, to be enjoyed now, enabling us to be of service to Jesus Christ in the time we have remaining in this world.

God saved you by his grace when you believed. And you can't take credit for this; it is a gift from God. Salvation is not a reward

for the good things we have done, so none of us can boast about it.
—Ephesians 2:8–9, NLT

For this is how God loved the world: He gave his one and only Son, so that everyone who believes in him will not perish but have eternal life.
—John 3:16, NLT

Whoever believes in the Son has eternal life; whoever does not obey the Son shall not see life, but the wrath of God remains on him.
—John 3:36, ESV

So it is with you. When you heard the true teaching—the Good News about your salvation—you believed in Christ. And in Christ, God put his special mark of ownership on you by giving you the Holy Spirit that he had promised. That Holy Spirit is the guarantee that we will receive what God promised for his people until God gives full freedom to those who are his—to bring praise to God's glory.
—Ephesians 1:13–14, NCV

Here I am! I stand at the door and knock. If anyone hears my voice and opens the door, I will come in and eat with that person, and they with me.
—Revelation 3:20

> I tell you the truth, those who listen to my message and believe in God who sent me have eternal life. They will never be condemned for their sins, but they have already passed from death into life.
>
> —John 5:24, NLT

This is wonderful news! Our sin has been paid for on the cross, our salvation is secure, and we have passed from death to life—a life that now can echo into eternity.

More Resources and Phil's Bio

If you found this book to be helpful in your spiritual life, be sure to also read Phil's book *KingdomNomics: Enjoy a Life That Will Echo into Eternity*. You can download it for free when you sign up for Phil's devotional series at www.KingdomNomics.com. These devotions have been prepared to help you reflect even more upon your use of the time, talent, and treasure that God has entrusted to you.

The repercussions of the decisions that you make today will echo into eternity. Continue to stay focused and fuel your passion for living for Christ as you use all that you have to glorify him.

Here are some additional resources that are available on the website:

The *KingdomNomics Applied* book will help you discover principles that can help you become a wise steward of your time, talent, and treasure. These thirty-one life-transforming devotions will help you:

- Discover how to use all of your resources strategically to glorify God.
- Become more heavenly minded and earthly sensitive.
- Experience the benefits of joyfully trading earthly, temporary gratification for something that will last forever.

The *KingdomNomics Study Guide* has been developed for use by individuals and small groups as a companion piece to the *KingdomNomics* book.

Phil also has a weekly blog, called "Reflections of a Kingdom Boy," where he shares more insights about how to create your own echo into eternity. See his latest blog posts at KingdomNomics.com/blog.

To access these resources, check out the KingdomNomics website at KingdomNomics.com and the Facebook page at facebook.com/KingdomNomics.

Phil has spent a lifetime learning about and living out the answer to this single question: *How can I enjoy life now, and still live a life that will echo into eternity?* He is the former CEO and President of T.W. Phillips Gas and Oil Co., and Phillips Resources Inc. (recently purchased by Exxon Mobil Corp.).

Phil graduated from Harvard University and the University of Pittsburgh School of Law. He knows what it is to make wise business decisions and to reap the benefits of those choices. In addition, he has learned what it means to make wise choices in regard to the use of personal wealth and how every choice can reap an eternal dividend.

CPSIA information can be obtained
at www.ICGtesting.com
Printed in the USA
LVOW01*1932101215
464363LV00001B/1/P